**WATERFORD
COUNTY MUSEUM**
Iarsmalann Contae Phort Láirge

Published by

WATERFORD
COUNTY MUSEUM
Iarsmalann Contae Phort Láirge

www.waterfordmuseum.ie

The Towns & Villages of the

Waterford Greenway

A history of Dungarvan, Abbeyside, Stradbally, Kilmacthomas, Portlaw & Waterford City

Authors
Eddie Cantwell, Ger Crotty, Cian Flaherty, William Fraher, Christina Knight-O'Connor, Cian Manning, Seán and Síle Murphy, Julian Walton, Martin Whelan and Willie Whelan

Photographers
Eamonn Bolger, John Foley and Pat Kenealy

Illustrators
Michael Power and Anne Lannon Power

Proofing and editing
Cian Flaherty, William Fraher, Julian Walton and Willie Whelan

Contents

Introduction

The Waterford Greenway is a spectacular 46 km off-road cycling and walking trail along the route of the old Waterford, Dungarvan and Lismore Railway line. The railway opened for passengers on 12 August 1878. The last scheduled train service departed Dungarvan Station on 25 March 1967. Over years of neglect the line became an overgrown, redundant, historical footnote. Spotting the potential of the disused line, local volunteer organisations such as the Déise Greenway Group campaigned for several years for it to be turned into a community amenity. Waterford City and County Council under the leadership of CEO Michael Walsh drove the project to completion and the Waterford Greenway was finally opened on 25 March 2017.

This book, chronicling the history of the localities surrounding the Greenway, is the result of work by four heritage groups, eleven historians, three photographers and two illustrators over a two-year period. All profits from this book are being donated to Portlaw Heritage Centre, Stradbally Church Ruins Committee, Waterford Archaeological and Historical Society and Waterford County Museum.

This book is a project of

Portlaw Heritage Centre

Stradbally Church Ruins Committee

Waterford Archaeological and Historical Society

Waterford County Museum

Thanks to the Waterford County Museum Committee, Waterford Leader Partnership, Waterford City and County Council, Dungarvan and West Waterford Chamber of Commerce, Printmaster, CMT CE Scheme, Irish Railway Record Society, Waterford Museum of Treasures, Jimmy Taaffe, Richie Walsh, Joanne Rothwell, Bernadette Guest, Rachael Power, Michael Fitzgerald, Tara McAndrew, Andy Kelly, Michael J. Walsh, Jenny Beresford, Pat Whyte, Val Mangan and Marcin Boreysza.

This project was initiated and managed for Waterford County Museum by Willie Whelan.

Finding places

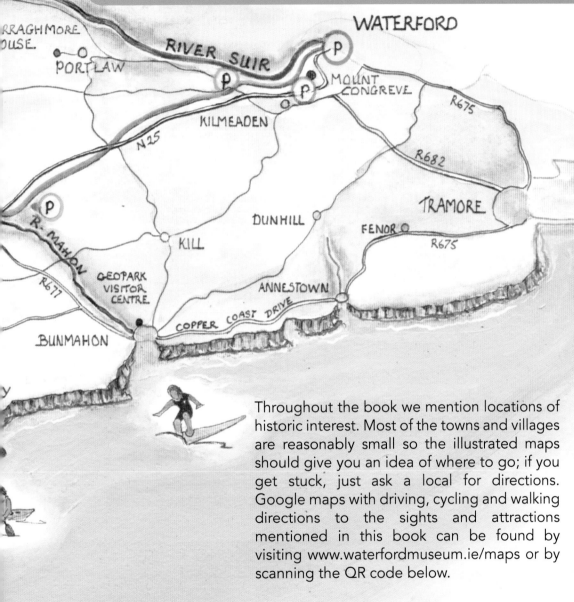

Throughout the book we mention locations of historic interest. Most of the towns and villages are reasonably small so the illustrated maps should give you an idea of where to go; if you get stuck, just ask a local for directions. Google maps with driving, cycling and walking directions to the sights and attractions mentioned in this book can be found by visiting www.waterfordmuseum.ie/maps or by scanning the QR code below.

Waterford Greenway Route Map

0   2.5   5   7.5   10 K.

DUNGARVAN

Founded in 1185 when Prince John commissioned Dungarvan Castle.

*T*he Dungarvan area has seen occupation in the Late Stone Age, Bronze Age and Early Christian period. Two fine Iron Age axes were found at Carraig Mhuiris cave, Whitechurch, near Dungarvan.

A legacy of the Iron Age are the numerous ogham stones to be found at Drumlohan, Ardmore, Ballyquin, Kilgrovan and elsewhere. Around the 3rd century a Celtic tribe called the Decie were dispossessed of their lands in Tara, Co. Meath and settled in this area and westward as far as the Cork border. This area is still known as Na nDéise (the Decies in English).

St Garvan is credited with founding the original settlement of Dungarvan. He was a disciple of St Finbarr and is known to have founded the monastery of Achadh Gharbháin in the 7th century, but it is disputed whether or not this refers to Dungarvan.

Recent excavations have revealed that there was a small Viking settlement at Shandon on the banks of the River Colligan, to the north of the present town. A carved bone trial piece from the 9th or 10th century was found during quarrying at Shandon in 1917. The artefact, 10 cm in length, features elements from both Gaelic and Viking traditions. Carved in the Scandinavian Jellinge style you can make out dragons on the piece if you look closely. It is now held in the National Museum of Ireland. The designs on the trial piece show how the Gaelic and Norse traditions were starting to influence each other after over 200 years of cultural cohabitation. It is thought that these trial pieces may have been a sort of 'sketch pad' used by craftsmen and their apprentices to experiment with design and layout before transferring their work to precious metal.

The town of Dungarvan really owes its foundation and development to the Anglo-Normans in the 13th century. Dungarvan became a royal honor in 1204. On 31 August that year Domhnall Ó Faoláin, King of the Decie, surrendered the province of Dungarvan to King John:

The King to Meyler FitzHenry, Justiciary of Ireland. Donald Uffeld [Ó Faoláin] having quit-claimed to the King the province of Dungarvan, one of three cantreds held by him, the King commands the justiciary to take that province into the King's hand, and cause the villeins and fugitives therefrom with their chattels and retinue to return. Donald shall hold the other two cantreds on his giving hostages for faithful service.

This is an important document recording the formal passing of Dungarvan from Gaelic to royal ownership. While a borough (a town or district with its own council) appears to have been already established at this time, the transfer of the town into royal ownership would have boosted the development of the existing settlement.

The Anglo-Normans erected a motte-and-bailey fortification at Gallows Hill to the west of the town and constructed a substantial castle through which they could control the port.

Another important development was the granting of a charter by King John on 3 July 1215. In the 13th century Dungarvan was becoming a prosperous settlement. The Exchequer returns for 1262-3 indicate that it was a town of considerable wealth and prosperity. It was trading with England, especially Bristol, and with the Continent, although it was not as important as other southern ports such as Youghal.

The most important export from Dungarvan was fish, which was sent to Liverpool, Chester and Bristol, among other places. Indeed, the majority of the population were employed in various aspects of the fishing industry and the Dungarvan fishermen were noted for their expertise in making nets. There was a pattern of fishing net in Cornwall known as the Dungarvan pattern; fishermen were brought over from Dungarvan to teach the locals how to make it.

An important boost to the town's development was the grant from Parliament in 1463:

As the Seignory of Dungarvan was the most great and antient honour belonging to the King in Ireland, which through war etc., was for the most part destroyed ... it was ordained that the Portreeve [Mayor] and Commonalty ... may have and enjoy all manner of free grants, liberties, privileges and customs as the tenants and inhabitants of the honourable Manor of Clare in England ... with a further power to take customs of all kinds of merchandise bought and sold within the franchises, as the Mayor and Commons of Bristol did, the profits to go to the reparation of the walls and towers under the survey of the Earl of Desmond...

The town wall was to be 16 feet high and 3 to 4 feet in thickness or alternatively 'a sufficient deep fosse [ditch] with a high bank' could be constructed. In the 16th century Dungarvan was attacked several times. In 1525 the Earl of Ormond burned the town while invading the Earl of Desmond's territory during the Desmond Rebellion. In 1526 Dungarvan was described as 'a great place of resort for English and other fishers'. In 1569 the author Edmund Campion noted: 'Dungarvan and Waterford full of traffic with England, France and Spain'.

002. Women known as 'Joulters' selling fish in Dungarvan c.1900.

In 1582 most of the buildings in the town were again destroyed by the Irish rebels. As a result of this destruction the town went into economic decline. The trades of the inhabitants noted in 1583 were mostly unskilled and agriculture-based, for example fishermen, yeomen, butchers, etc.; one goldsmith is mentioned. There was a notable lack of skilled craftsmen and mercantile trades.

The town received a new charter of incorporation as a borough from King James I in 1610. In 1611 Dungarvan was described as 'a poor fishertown of which the chief trade [was] fish taken there'.

Dungarvan featured prominently in the Eleven Years War of the mid-17th-century. In March 1642 Sir William St Leger, Lord President of Munster, attacked the town and many of the citizens were killed. Soon after, the castle was retaken by the Irish.

Over the next few years Dungarvan became one of the Confederates' (Irish rebels) main ports and ships were sent

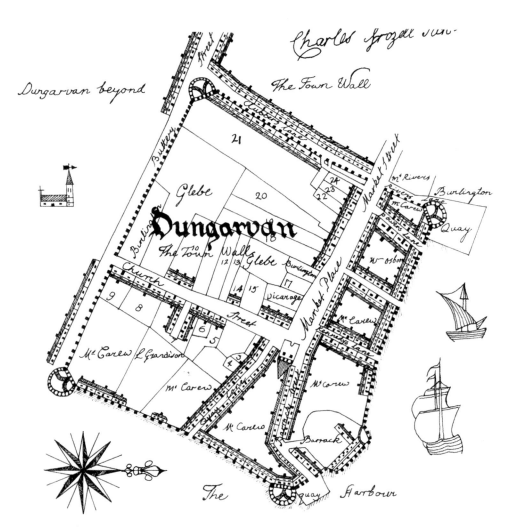

003. A map of Dungarvan showing the town walls in 1760.

to Spain and other places for arms and supplies. In 1647 Lord Inchiquin attacked Dungarvan but only recaptured it after a fierce siege lasting several days, which destroyed the town. Sir Philip Perceval commented the same year that there were 'no inhabitants or stuff in any of the houses'.

Oliver Cromwell reached Dungarvan on 4 December 1649. However, the town had surrendered the day before to Lord Broghill who gave the following account of the event: 'The 2nd of this month with a party of 600 horse and 800 foot, I advanced to Dungarvan, where the Lord so ruled their hearts that on the 3rd it was delivered up to me by Colonel Kinsale … there was in the town 6 ordnance, 16 barrels of powder with bullet and match proportionable'.

Cromwell set up his headquarters in Youghal. His lieutenant general, Michael

004. A soldier of the Irish Catholic Confederation with a demi-pike, 1640s.

Jones, stayed on in a house in Church Street, Dungarvan, as he was ill with a fever. Cromwell recalled this illness: 'I scarcely know an officer of forty amongst us, that hath not been sick … The noble Lieutenant General … fell sick … struggling for some four or five days with a fever, he died'. Jones died on 10 December and was buried in Youghal. There is a local legend which states that the town was saved from destruction by the actions of a Mrs Nagle who drank to Cromwell's health and offered refreshments to his men.

Extrapolating data from Petty's Census of 1659 suggests Dungarvan's approximate population was 1,278. The town's charter was renewed in 1689. The corporation allowed this charter to lapse in the mid-18th century when the arms and seal were also lost.

Throughout the 17th century Dungarvan continued to be noted for its fish which were widely exported. A major obstacle to the development of trade was the lack of an adequate quay coupled with the layout of the harbour. In the 1680s the Revd Arthur Stanhope wrote the following description of Dungarvan: 'Dungarvan which lies open to the sea requires a skilfull pilot for bringing ships up to the town, because of a dangerous Barr that lies neare the mouth of the harbour. Great store of fish here taken, as cod, ling, hake etc., and sent into foreign parts'.

At the beginning of the 18th century the town was in a state of decay, without a sufficient water supply or quay. In 1752 Richard Pococke (traveller, author and later Bishop of Ossory) described it as a 'good fishing town and famous for the export of potatoes to many parts of Ireland'. In the late 18th century it was described as a small seaport with little trade and inhabited mostly by fishermen. All this was to change with the reconstruction of Dungarvan by the 5th and 6th Dukes of Devonshire at the beginning of the 19th century. The Devonshires had acquired their Irish property in 1748 on the marriage of Charlotte, daughter of the 3rd Earl of Burlington and 4th Earl of Cork, to William Cavendish, later 4th Duke of Devonshire.

The 6th Duke of Devonshire, William Spencer Cavendish (1790-1858), inherited the family estates on the death

005. William Spencer Cavendish, 6th Duke of Devonshire (1790-1858).

of his father in 1811. He supported Catholic emancipation, the abolition of slavery and reduced working hours for factory workers. He was a great collector and had a keen interest in horticulture.

In Dungarvan, the Devonshires began to buy up adjoining properties in order to create a new town centre, quay and marketplace. The architect William Atkinson was commissioned to draw up the plans. The work took place between 1803 and 1830. Jesse Hartley (designer of the Liverpool docks) was appointed engineer for the project. While based in Dungarvan Hartley married Ellen, daughter of the seneschal William Penny.

The development transformed the look of the town and created a new era of prosperity. This work included a spacious new square called Devonshire Square (now Grattan Square), fish and meat markets and a new bridge over the River Colligan to connect the town with the village of Abbeyside. A substantial new quay was also built which was a major boost to shipping and commerce. Dungarvan had its own shipbuilding industry in the 18th and 19th centuries. It is thought that the boats were constructed above the old railway bridge near where the civic offices are now. The shipbuilders included Mahoney, Risbill, Kidney, Thompson, Large and Power. A report of 1832 noted that Dungarvan was in a 'prosperous and improving state, [and was] neat in appearance and a popular sea resort'. The fisheries were still a major source of employment for about 4,000 of the town's inhabitants.

In 1839 construction began on a workhouse (now Dungarvan Community Hospital) to a design by George Wilkinson; it was completed in 1841.

It was situated at the Spring to the west of the town. The workhouse was constructed to accommodate 600 inmates. At the height of the Famine, in 1847, almost 2,000 people were living in this workhouse. As the Famine progressed and the scale of the disaster became obvious, additional auxiliary workhouses were rented around Dungarvan to accommodate an additional 2,000 'paupers'. Several thousand more were dependent on food handouts, known as outdoor relief, to survive. It is difficult to describe the horrendous impact of the Famine to a modern person. The absence of film or photographs and the passage of time has led to its fading from memory. The scenes around the town would

006. The Dungarvan coat of arms on a postcard dated 1907.

19

007. The earliest known image of Dungarvan, 1746.

007. *The earliest known image of Dungarvan, 1746.*

have been comparable to those of the Ethiopian famine of the 1980s. Such was the pressure to accommodate the starving that the shop counters in Boyle's house (an auxiliary workhouse) were removed to allow the 200 girl inmates lie down to sleep. Within the workhouse system family units were broken up on admission and men, women and children were accommodated separately.

During this time people were buried at Kilrush until a special cemetery was opened in 1847 at Slievegrine. Mass burials in unmarked graves were common. The Famine period had a disastrous effect on the town, drastically reducing the population, and those who could afford it emigrated, never to return. From a population high of 10,000 in 1840, the town shrank to contain around 5,000 inhabitants in the 1920s.

In 1854 the Towns Improvement Act was adopted and town commissioners were elected. The modern Dungarvan coat of arms dates from 1863 and was designed by William Williams to replace an earlier, lost coat of arms. Williams explained the design:

008. Irish cycling pioneer Richard Edward Brenan (1846-1917), c.1895.

009. *Ireland's first cycling club, the Dungarvan Ramblers, c.1900.*

The castles of the shield are ... portraits of existing structures, as they appeared about a century since. That to the left is the Dun or castle of Abbeyside ... That to the right represents a wing of the old ... Dungarvan castle. Between the castles is seen a ship in full sail approaching the harbour ... Our supporters are two ancient Irish warriors wearing the National costume and armed with the National weapons of other days. Our crest, an anchor and dolphin entwined, and our motto, taken in its literal sense, are all indicative of the maritime situation of the town. Our motto – 'Ní Maraide Go Stiúrthóir' – 'Not a Mariner Till a Steersman' is intended to teach an important moral lesson. Individually we are admonished, such that we make ourselves acquainted with the duties of our various callings, in order that we may be able to direct our own affairs, and collectively that, if we desire to see the town satisfactorily governed, we must grasp the reins with our own hand...

In the 1860s the town began to recover and prosper somewhat. Several new buildings were constructed and a gasworks established. In 1872 the Waterford, Dungarvan and Lismore Railway (WD&LR) was incorporated using £280,000 share capital plus a £93,333 loan from the Treasury, and this funding was used to construct the railway line between Lismore and Waterford city. In 1878 the Waterford, Dungarvan and Lismore Railway was officially opened and this helped to develop the economy of the town. The town's first urban district council was established in April 1899.

The Dungarvan Ramblers Cycle Club was founded in 1869 by Richard Edward Brenan (1846-1917). This was the first such club in Ireland. Brenan

010. British forces leaving Dungarvan, 4 March 1922.

was a postmaster, bookseller and photographer who had his business premises in Grattan Square. In 1869 the club organised the first cycle race for a challenge cup held in Ireland or Britain. The race was held in Dungarvan and Brenan was the winner. Brenan won the race again in 1870 and 1871. In 1868 Brenan went on what is believed to be the first documented Irish cycle holiday, to Co. Cork.

The town went into commercial decline towards the end of the 19th century. However, it became increasingly popular as a sea resort and a new esplanade and park were created using a bequest from Captain William Gibbons.

On 4 March 1922, Dungarvan Castle was surrendered to the IRA. For the first time in over 700 years the town would not be governed from England. Local historian Edmond Keohan left an eyewitness account of events:

All the police from the west of the county, as well as from several stations in East Cork, had been drafted into Dungarvan [Castle] for security, and their force numbered 65 at this time ... They were under the command of Captain Sheehan, an officer who had fought in the Great War ... He formed his men four deep in the square, and giving the order 'March', the men filed out of the Castle, passed through the massive gateway, and thus was ended, apparently for evermore, the symbol of British rule in this historic fortress...

There were many onlookers at their doors and windows as the body of police marched up the street, headed by their Captain, en route for the railway station, to leave the

011. West Waterford IRA occupy Dungarvan Castle, 4 March 1922.

old town for ever. Some of the men smiled greetings to their friends as they passed them by, others appeared to realise the changed position of affairs. A musical instrument was being played by one of the party, and the air 'Good-Bye-ee' only indicated too well the meaning of the proceeding. Their departure was regarded with mixed feelings, and perhaps at the moment the mind was filled with kindly recollections. For, until the strife, these men and the public had got on very well together...

It might have been two hours later that three motor cars drove down the street. In them were members of the IRA. They entered the barracks and installed themselves there, and within a few minutes the Tricolour floated from the ramparts of the building. These incidents in themselves were of tremendous significance, in as much as they emphasised the change that had taken place, that the rule of which the people had so long complained was at an end, and that the affairs of the country were now in the hands of their own representatives.

The chief trade from Dungarvan port in the early 1900s was in the export of timber and corn. Dower's Brewery was one of the major employers. It was run by John R. Dower. In 1919 Thomas Power purchased the brewery from the Marquess of Waterford and developed it further. He also started producing cider and jam. In 1917 the Shandon Dairy employed over 100 men. It was eventually acquired by the Dungarvan Co-operative Creamery Ltd (established

012. *The 1798 monument and Victorian bandstand in Dungarvan Town Park.*

013. Grattan Square, Dungarvan.

1921) which produced milk powder, milk foods and baby foods and operated a sawmill. In 1964 Dungarvan Co-op brought together four of the county's five co-ops to form Waterford Co-op, and the name was changed to Waterford Foods. It is now part of Glanbia. The Dungarvan factory closed in 1996.

In 1935 a major new industry was started in Dungarvan, the Dickens Leather Company Ltd, which produced leather boot and shoe linings and leather for bookbinding, sandals etc. Waterford Crystal opened a branch in Dungarvan in 1972 and for forty years it was the town's main employer until it shut in

2006. Throughout the 1990s Dungarvan expanded rapidly with many new building projects. The cultural life of the town is well catered for with the Library, County Archive, Museum, Theatre and Arts Centre. The key historical building in the town, Dungarvan Castle, has been restored by Dúchas and is open to the public.

On 25 March 2017, Waterford Council held the official opening of the Waterford Greenway, a cycle and pedestrian route between Dungarvan and Waterford. Fittingly, it was fifty years after the last passenger train on the line ran on 25 March 1967.

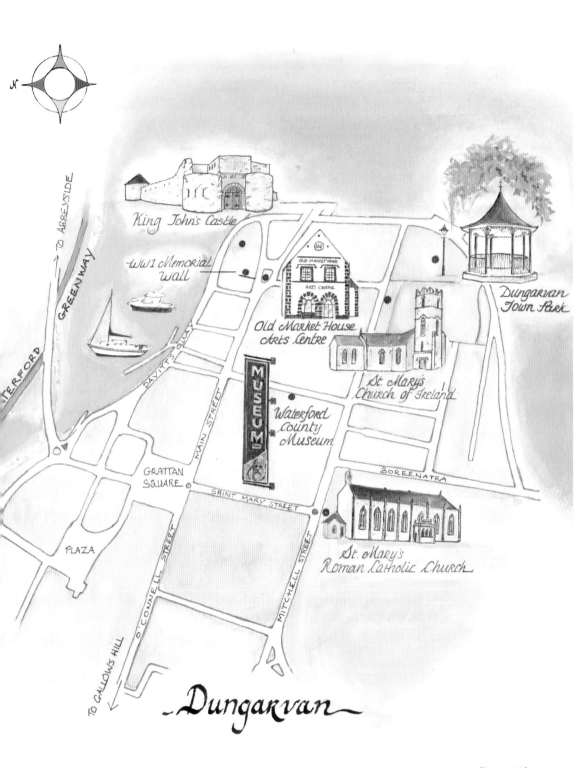

N

TO ABBEYSIDE

GREENWAY

WATERFORD

King John's Castle

WW1 Memorial Wall

DAVITT'S QUAY

MAIN STREET

MUSEUM

GRATTAN SQUARE

PLAZA

O CONNELL STREET

TO GALLOWS HILL

SAINT MARY STREET

MITCHELL STREET

OLD MARKET HOUSE

1641

ART CENTRE

Old Market House Arts Centre

Waterford County Museum

St. Mary's Church of Ireland

BOREENATRA

St. Mary's Roman Catholic Church

Dungarvan Town Park

Dungarvan

0   50   100   150   200m

014. Map of Dungarvan.

015. Market day in Grattan Square, Dungarvan, c.1900.

Grattan Square

The square that is at the heart of modern day Dungarvan is named after the Irish politician Henry Grattan (1746–1820). Grattan was a member of the Irish House of Commons who campaigned for legislative freedom for the Irish Parliament in the late 18th century.

This spacious square of one acre dates from the early 19th century when the town was reconstructed by the 5th and 6th Dukes of Devonshire. In 1801 it was decided to develop the Devonshire property in Dungarvan. A large building programme was initiated which would create forty-shilling freeholders entitled to vote in parliamentary elections. Those who obtained new houses were expected to vote for the Duke's candidate at election time, thereby increasing his influence in the town.

By 1806 properties on the site of the proposed square had been demolished and a new square and surrounding streets were being laid out. Welsh slate, Yorkshire flags and Portland stone were imported from Britain. The houses on the square were of three storeys and had a limestone parapet. On the north side, flanking the entrance to Bridge Street, were two four-storey buildings. The architect of these improvements was William Atkinson who also carried out improvements at Lismore Castle. Engineer and architect Jesse Hartley (designer of the Liverpool docks) was brought over from Yorkshire to supervise the work on the square and bridge. While based in Dungarvan Hartley married Ellen, daughter of the seneschal William Penny.

Since the grant of the town charter by King John in 1215, Dungarvan has been a market town. 'Market town' is a legal term, originating in the Middle Ages, for a settlement that has the right to host markets, distinguishing it from a village and city. In 1242 Henry III granted Dungarvan the right to hold a yearly fair. The original name of the square was Market Square. By the mid 19th century it was called Devonshire Square before finally being renamed Grattan Square. The original purpose of the square was to hold a market so that all the local farmers and traders could sell their goods.

The square was the scene of a dramatic episode in Ireland's Civil War in March 1922. General Michael Collins, Commander-in-Chief of the National Army, was delivering a political speech from the back of a lorry when the lorry was hijacked by three young Republicans in an attempt to kidnap him. The vehicle was driven out of the square along Bridge Street in the direction of Abbeyside and was only stopped when a gun was held to the head of the driver. The driver leaped out of the lorry while it was still moving and managed to escape under fire from Collins' bodyguards.

The surface of Grattan Square was modernised in 2016. At the threshold of each business premises around the Square is an engraved stone plaque commemorating people, events and industry from Dungarvan's past. You can download a PDF file detailing the story behind each plaque at www.waterfordmuseum.ie.

The Old Market House

One of the town's most historic buildings, the Old Market House terminates the view down Church Street and Parnell Street. The Old Market House has been reconstructed to house an arts centre. The distinctive black and white main front has two arches. A charter of 1610

016. Main Street (Parnell Street), Dungarvan, c.1910.

instructed the Corporation to erect a stone guildhall as soon as possible. A town hall was in existence in 1642 when its capture is recorded. It seems likely that the present building incorporates parts of this town hall. Rebuilt in the early 18th century as a butter market and town hall, it had an open arcade on three sides and a small cupola on the roof.

According to local tradition, Edmond Power was hanged from a window of the building in 1799. He was also drawn and quartered, his head being left in Dungarvan gaol and his body buried in Kilgobnet churchyard. Power was one of the local yeomanry but was also secretly a member of the United Irishmen. The Society of United Irishmen was a revolutionary republican organisation, inspired by the American Revolution and allied with revolutionary France. The United Irishmen launched the Irish Rebellion of 1798 with the objective of ending British rule over Ireland and founding an independent Irish republic.

To the left of the Old Market House is a three-storey building. A commemorative plaque on the house records it as the place where James F.X. O'Brien was born in 1828. After studying medicine in Dublin, O'Brien went to America where he took part in the American Civil War, working as an assistant surgeon. On his return to Ireland he joined the Fenian movement. The Fenians were a secret oath-bound organisation dedicated to the establishment of an independent Irish republic in the 19th and early 20th centuries. Fenianism's two main principles were first, that Ireland had a natural right to independence, and second, that that right could be won only by an armed revolution. Because of his involvement in the Fenian Rising against British rule in 1867 O'Brien was arrested and sentenced to death. However, his sentence was commuted to penal servitude for life. In later life he became a Member of Parliament for South Mayo and Cork.

Also near the Old Market House is the Waterford World War I memorial unveiled on 6 October 2013. This memorial commemorates the 1,100 Waterford people who died in the First World War – it lists the name and place of origin of each casualty. Approximately half of the individuals named on the wall have no known grave.

King John's Castle

Prince John arrived in Waterford in 1185 and initiated the building of a number of castles in the south-east of Ireland, including the one at Dungarvan. By 1209 a stone castle had been erected at the mouth of the harbour. The castle has a polygonal keep and a twin-towered gatehouse. At the western corner there is a large two-storey tower. At its base the castle wall is over seven feet thick. The massive southern wall with its walkway still survives and gives some indication of the original strength of the castle. In the centre of the yard are the remains of the old military barracks, built in the 18th century. An inquisition of 1299 states that: 'there are at Dungarvan a castle in bad repair, unroofed, and nearly levelled to the ground, a new tower unroofed, a stone house beyond the gate in ill condition'.

The castle was taken over by the Earl of Ossory and the Lord Deputy in 1535 and thereafter became a royal castle once again. The castle was badly damaged in the Desmond Rebellion, which began

017. King John's Castle was built to control Dungarvan harbour.

018. King John's Castle from the air.

in 1579. In 1580 it was described as being 'in extreme ruin' and its repair was ordered in 1582.

In 1594 Henry Dockwray was appointed Constable with a wage of four shillings a day for himself. The castle garrison consisted of six archers on a wage of sixpence a day and fifteen foot soldiers paid eightpence a day.

The castle played a major role in the Eleven Years War. In 1641 Dungarvan rebelled along with most other towns in Munster. In March 1642 Sir William St Leger took the town which was burned,

with many of the townspeople being killed. A Lieutenant Rossington was left in charge of the castle. However, the Irish rebels soon recaptured the castle, led by Richard Butler of Kilcash, John FitzGerald of Farnane and John Hore FitzMathew and his son. The castle was taken in the following manner (John Hore had borrowed a ladder from the castle some weeks before on the pretence of repairing the roof of his house at Shandon):

Hore sent word to the said Castle to fetch in the said lather. For, saith he, 'the enemy is neere at hand, and it is to be feared they

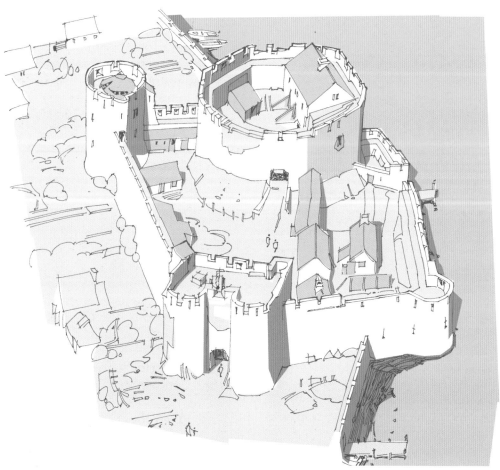

019. King John's Castle in the 1640s.

will scale the walls except it were brought in by times, and withal sent six men with the ladder to the castle gate; and presently noe sooner were the gates open to receive in the ladder but the parties that carried the same stood in the middest of the said gate with the one half of the ladder within doors and thother half without'. Whereby the rebels instantly rushed in a great number and took the said castle.

Lord Inchiquin arrived in Dungarvan on 3 May 1647 and tried for four days to make a breach in the town walls. On 10 May the garrison surrendered to Inchiquin. The castle was eventually taken by negotiation rather than by force. A contemporary account notes that:

The Soldiers are enraged that they had so good terms as was given them. They marched out from all these Garrisons with their Arms, Colours flying, Drums beating, Bullet in Mouth, their Goods and Provisions. The Rebels made two sallies out of Dungarvan, a Seaport and a walled Town, in half an hour, and killed two of our Captains and some others; after we had possession of the Castle which stands close to the Town, and deprived the Rebels from Water, they surrendered it on the same terms. But some twenty English men of the Red-Coats, that had run to the Rebels, that were taken in the several Garrisons, were hanged.

Inchiquin stated that he saw Dungarvan 'so strong that ... an army no better provided than we were might have been kept out of it until their own wants should enforce their surrender'.

In the first half of the 18th century the castle was rebuilt as an infantry barracks. The last soldiers to occupy the barracks were the King's Own Borderers who left in 1882. It was then taken over by the Royal Irish Constabulary. They evacuated the barracks in March 1922 and it was taken over by the IRA. The Free State troops took Dungarvan in August 1922, but before leaving the Republicans set fire to the castle, so making a dramatic exit from the town. The castle served as a Garda barracks until the 1980s. It opened to the public in 2002.

Dungarvan Town Park

Overlooking Dungarvan Bay is a beautiful Victorian town park laid out in 1894. The entrance from Park Terrace is through an archway which has a stone to the memory of Captain William Gibbons, who donated money for the setting out of the park. Originally this plaque contained the names of the Dungarvan Town Commissioners. The Commissioners were responsible for the administration of the town but at this period in history they were infamous for being argumentative, corrupt and self-interested. The inclusion of their names so incensed Captain Gibbons' widow, Mary Gibbons, that she contacted the Commissioners asking them to remove the plaque or she would take legal action. In November 1894 the plaque was finally taken down from over the archway. The current inscription was added to the blank side of the plaque and the side containing the names of the Town Commissioners was put facing into the wall. Before the plaque's removal the names of the Town Commissioners had been crossed out in paint by a disapproving local. This plaque is known as 'the Condemned Slab'.

Standing on the bandstand, there is a magnificent view of the bay. The sand spit, known as the Cunnigar, projects into the bay. The two headlands at the

020. The bandstand in Dungarvan Town Park c.1900.

entrance to the bay are Ballinacourty Point on the left and Helvick Head on the right. Across the harbour, in Abbeyside, you can see the remains of the old Augustinian abbey which was built c.1290. The cast-iron bandstand was erected c.1900 and made by MacFarlane's of Glasgow. Here on many summer evenings tourists known locally as 'Gaybricks' and Dungarvan residents enjoyed the music of the brass band. Also in the park is a monument in the form of a Celtic cross. The cross was erected in 1903 to the memory of Edmond Power who was hanged at the Market House in 1799 for being a member of the United Irishmen.

St Mary's Church of Ireland Church

The churchyard of St Mary's is hidden from view by a very old stone wall, which faces onto Emmet Street. The entrance gates and piers, which still survive, were erected in 1795 at a cost of £12. The present church was rebuilt to a design by James Pain c.1828. It incorporates part of an earlier church of c.1700. The church has a T-plan and is built of limestone ashlar. The windows have simple Gothic-style timber frames. An extension was added to the east end in 1903, and also in this period new stained-glass windows were installed by Watsons of Youghal.

A curious feature to the west of the church is the old gable wall with its five circular windows. This wall is about 32

021. Pupils of St Mary's Church of Ireland School, Dungarvan, c.1910.

feet long and 30 feet high, the windows being of dressed sandstone. After much research it now seems certain this wall is all that remains of the old pre-Reformation parish church of St Mary the Virgin, records of which date back to the 14th century. In 1642, during the Eleven Years War, the Irish rebels under a Captain Fennell destroyed the interior of the church and used it as a stable and prison for the Protestant inhabitants.

This church was described by historian Charles Smith in 1746:

Formerly the Parish Church was a large building, with a high steeple, but the whole was demolished by Cromwell. It is at present rebuilt where the chancel of the old church stood, the banks of the churchyard are washed by the ocean at high water the same being handsomely laid out into gravel walks planted with trees.

The beautiful view from here, much admired by 18th- and 19th-century visitors to Dungarvan, can still be appreciated today. There is a very large graveyard with many interesting old gravestones. The path through the churchyard was an ancient right of way for the fishermen of Boreenatra to their boats on the quay. On the west side of the cemetery near the path is a memorial erected to mark the site of the mass grave of those who were drowned after the wreck of the Moresby in Dungarvan harbour in 1895.

The small neo-Tudor house in the corner of the churchyard is the old Church of Ireland school built in 1846.

St Mary's Roman Catholic Church

St Mary's was one of the largest Catholic churches built in Ireland in the early 19th century. The church so dwarfed the nearby Protestant church (also called St Mary's) that certain members of the local Protestant community, including the Duke of Devonshire's agent, were very much opposed to its construction. The agent's objections were overruled by the 6th Duke of Devonshire who donated the land and also contributed £1,500 to the cost of the building. The Duke makes for an intriguing character as he confounds some of the expectations people have about the landlord class. He campaigned against slavery – not a particularly brave stance in a modern context, but at the time Waterford had pro- and anti-slavery newspapers, many Waterford people were very concerned about the effect abolition would have on the cotton mills at Portlaw, and it was not uncommon for many business- and ship-owners to support the Confederacy in the American Civil War. In the face of much opposition the Duke also campaigned for Catholic emancipation. This local opposition to Catholic emancipation came to the fore during the construction of St Mary's Parish Church.

It was a very ambitious undertaking for a relatively small town and as a result the original plans were never executed in full. A tower was planned for the west end, which would have made an attractive addition to the town's skyline, but unfortunately lack of money prevented its construction.

The building was designed by George Richard Pain of Cork and was finally completed and opened in 1828. The exterior is simply designed with slender limestone buttresses. The pattern of the stone tracery is different in each window. The elaborate east window and the west porch were added in the late 19th century. The building was altered and renovated under the direction of the parish priest Fr Cleary in the 1870s. He removed the old balconies, stone floor etc., and installed new stained-glass windows designed by Wailes & Strang of Newcastle-upon-Tyne. In the 1890s further improvements were made, including an entrance porch by George Ashlin.

Inside, the most attractive feature of the building is the beautiful neo-Gothic ceiling, which has ribbed vaulting, pendants and huge bosses down the centre of the nave. Beneath the main altar is a splendid sculpture entitled 'the Pietà'. It is carved in the style of the noted local sculptor John Hogan of Tallow but was executed by Scannell & Co of Cork.

Waterford County Museum

Since 1999, Dungarvan's old town hall has housed Waterford County Museum on the ground floor and the Town Hall Theatre on the first floor. Admission to the museum is free of charge. Originally the building was a late-18th-century grain store built by local merchant Thomas Buckley. It was converted to become Dungarvan's town hall in the 1870s. The ground floor had three open

022. St Mary's Roman Catholic Church.

arches where the butter market was held, and upstairs was a council chamber and theatre. The present unusual plaster front dates from the early 1900s.

The museum hosts a permanent display on the history of Co. Waterford and also runs occasional temporary exhibitions on other local history topics. It is run on a voluntary basis by the Waterford County Museum Society, founded as Dungarvan Museum Society in 1984. The Museum Society also publishes books and pamphlets on items of historical and local interest. The museum maintains an active presence on social media. We welcome all visitors including school groups. The museum does not do genealogical research but is happy to support people who are researching their Waterford ancestry. For museum opening hours please consult:
www.waterfordmuseum.ie
or email history@waterfordmuseum.ie.

Gallows Hill

Gallows Hill is a large mound that once dominated Dungarvan's landscape. Today it is completely obscured by housing developments. You do not get a sense of how commanding the view from it is unless you climb to the summit. The hill has endured decades of neglect, and its summit has suffered extensive damage due to annual bonfires. Down through the years many theories have been put forward regarding the origin of the mound – these have included a Norman motte (castle), a barrow (ancient burial mound), or a hill where a gallows was erected. Some documentation exists in various archives to support some of these theories. A hanging is documented on the hill in the 18th century. A cannonball recovered during an archaeological dig at the site may have rolled down from the hilltop. The cannonball could date from the Desmond Rebellion or the Eleven Years' War when Parliament, Royalists and Catholic Confederates fought a three-way battle for Ireland, with Dungarvan changing hands on numerous occasions. The hill is called 'Cromwell's Mound' in an old document, suggesting that it may have been part of siege works during the Eleven Years' War. The fortification seems to have been used to protect (or threaten) Dungarvan's water supply at St Bridget's Well (formerly known as Fort Well).

The steep profile of the original mound is typical of castle mottes of the 12th and 13th centuries, and with its strategic location Gallows Hill looks like a castle built to blockade, and lay siege to, the early town (and castle) of Dungarvan.

023. Old Market House, Dungarvan.

ABBEYSIDE

A 13th-century village that grew around an Augustinian monastery.

102. A view of *Abbeyside church from the sea, July 1966.*

*O*n the beginning there was the Augustinian priory. There were earlier ringfort settlements in the locality, but the genesis of what we now know as Abbeyside really began with the community of Augustinian friars that settled in the area c.1290. The Augustinian friars came into being as part of the mendicant movement of the 13th century, a new form of religious life which sought to bring the religious ideals of monastic life into an urban setting. They sought to tend to the spiritual and religious needs of the local community in which they lived, and fulfilled many of the functions we nowadays associate with parish priests.

The Augustinian influence in the locality survives to this day with St Augustine's College at Duckspool on the outskirts of Abbeyside. The Order of St Augustine still maintain a friary (built c.1870) and church (built c.1824) in Dungarvan town.

A modern visitor to the locality might incorrectly assume that Abbeyside was a suburb of Dungarvan. In fact, the village has its own distinct character and history. It is a well known fact that the simplest way to annoy an Abbeyside person is to ask them if they are from Dungarvan. This rivalry, which now mainly manifests itself on the sporting field, has a basis in history. For 500 years the town of Dungarvan and village of Abbeyside were two separate communities. When it came to fording Dungarvan harbour, the contrast between Dungarvan's reliance on ferry boats and Abbeyside's reliance on waiting for low tide helped foster clear-cut distinctions between the two settlements. Historically, Abbeyside had a much smaller population and was less prosperous. Villagers were generally reliant on a subsistence lifestyle of fishing and growing crops on their allotment or smallholding.

Abbeyside appears less frequently in the historical record than Dungarvan but during the Irish Confederate Wars (or Eleven Years' War, 1641-53), Abbeyside, along with Dungarvan and the rest of Munster, was to suffer greatly.

The conflict initially pitted the native Irish Catholics against English and Scottish Protestant colonists. It ended with Royalists, Irish Catholics and Scottish Presbyterians fighting the ultimate winners, the English Parliament. It was both a religious and an ethnic conflict – fought over who would govern Ireland, whether it would be governed from England, which ethnic and religious group would own most of the land, and which religion would predominate in the country. It was the most destructive conflict in Irish history. Comparisons could be drawn with the Syrian Civil War, in the drawn-out nature of the conflict, with shifting alliances and a patchwork quilt of territories changing hands frequently.

The Revd Urban Vigors wrote a letter dated 16 July 1642 with an account of the attack on Dungarvan by an English army under Sir William St Leger in March of that year:

Thursday morning being the 4th day of March, our army, between eight and nine of the clock, came close before the town of Dungarvan. We took it within three hours' fight, and burned most of the houses which were thatched, and burned likewise a stately stone house, well slated, of one Mr Hoare's [a known Confederate Rebel] adjoining the Town. There were divers gentlemen and others that escaped over the strand on

103. An Abbeyside hurling team from 1941.

horseback, the water being then fordable, for it was the beginning of the flood. [Where the quay stands in Dungarvan was once a beach. The harbour could be crossed at low tide.] My Lord President, perceiving it, caused a squadron of the best shots to make to the strand with all haste, which killed many of the Rebels [Catholic Confederates], notwithstanding many escaped. Whereupon my Lord caused a party of horse of every troop to be chosen out to ride to the other side of the river, and burn the town upon that side [Abbeyside] and kill as many as came over. We were forty horse upon that service. Captain George Welsh, who is now in this city, was with us, and behaved himself valiantly, and did good service to my own knowledge, for I was an eye-witness unto it. We burnt the town on that side the strand, according to our directions. There were killed by our party of horse, near fifty and I think there were killed and hanged the like number.

On the other side of the town [Dungarvan] were many killed and thrown into the sea. There is not any man, I dare say, can tell certainly how many were killed and drowned: some say 200, some 300, and some 400. But I am of [the] opinion 200 were the most that were slain ... Saturday morning the 5th of March they yielded up the Castle ... They could not have stood [held] out long, for our shot kept them from water. Those that were in the Castle [McGrath's Castle, Abbeyside] on the other side of the town had quarter to depart only with their lives and wearing clothes. There was a great store of pillage taken in the town by our soldiers, and a good quantity of excellent Spanish Iron...

104. A soldier of the Irish Catholic Confederation with a matchlock musket, 1640s.

In May 1647 Lord Inchiquin with a large English/Parliamentary army of 5,000 foot and 1,500 horse invaded the Confederate-controlled area of Co. Waterford. He arrived at Dungarvan on 3 May 1647. After four days he eventually breached the town walls of Dungarvan after a tower collapsed under artillery bombardment. The castle held out for another three days despite being under bombardment from elements of Inchiquin's forces in Abbeyside. A contemporary account describes the castle garrison launching a surprise attack across Dungarvan harbour at low tide to attack the Parliamentary cannon firing on the castle from Abbeyside. They surprised their foes and managed to destroy two of the cannon, killing two popular Roundhead officers. This setback meant that the Parliamentary forces were forced to grant 'quarter' to the garrison on 10 May, as they could no longer capture the castle quickly by force. A contemporary account notes that '[t]he [Parliamentary] Soldiers are enraged that they had so good terms as was given them. They marched out from all these Garrisons with their Arms, Colours flying, Drums beating, Bullet in Mouth, their Goods and Provisions...'

The Census of Ireland taken in 1659 gives the population of Abbeyside as forty-four; Dungarvan's was 213. Recent historical opinion is that these figures are a count of heads of household. Data from 1672 indicates that the number of people per household was between 5.5 and six. This would give a very rough population count of 1,278 for Dungarvan and 264 for Abbeyside. Perhaps the most valuable aspect of these figures is that they show the relative sizes of the village and the town.

Abbeyside had representatives on both sides of the 1798 Rebellion, a failed but bloody insurrection launched by the United Irishmen, an underground republican society, who wished to establish an Irish republic based on the principles of the French Revolution. In November 1797 Thomas Christopher of Abbeyside gathered with 800 United Irishmen in a field at Cushcam. They had planned to steal cannon from a privateer called the *Vulture* which was moored in Dungarvan harbour. They intended to use the cannon to blow up several country houses, especially Curraghmore, home of the Marquess of Waterford. On 4 January 1798 Michael Heffernan informed on Patrick Tagly, shoemaker of Abbeyside, who had approached him several times about stealing cannon from the *Vulture* and assisting in the murder of various gentlemen.

In April 1798 a meeting was held in Abbeyside, chaired by the parish priest, Fr James Power. The inhabitants of Abbeyside protested their loyalty and referred to the disturbances which had been lately ushered into their parish by incendiaries. They all undertook to inform against all whom they knew to be members of an unlawful assembly. A copy of the resolution was sent to the Marquess of Waterford.

The opening of the bridge and causeway connecting Dungarvan and Abbeyside in 1816 had an enormous impact on the development of Abbeyside. From the 1820s high-quality housing was constructed along Strandside in the now easily accessible village. What had primarily been a hamlet of fishermen and labourers saw an influx of the professional classes. The community that had once had the 13th-century Augustinian abbey

105. *The earliest known view of Abbeyside, by artist Anthony Chearnley c.1746.*

105. The earliest known view of Abbeyside, by artist Anthony Chearnley c.1746.

at its heart was now centred around the new bridge. The old road to Waterford city that ran along modern-day Sarsfield Street was usurped by a more direct route along Sexton Street that aligned with the newly built causeway.

An 1836 report by the Commissioners of Irish Fisheries gives an idea of the state of the life of the local fishermen. It also highlights the differences between the fishermen of Abbeyside and Dungarvan:

At Abbeyside ... most of the fishermen occupy small allotments of land and are comparatively thriving, prosperous and industrious. Their boats generally well found and themselves and families well clothed. They rarely ever want food, as the application ... to the portions of land which they hold, generally gives them an abundance, and the best moral effects are produced by constant employment and the want of time to go to the public house. On the western side [Dungarvan town] the fishermen have comfortable houses built for them by the Duke of Devonshire and are subject to only a nominal rent, but they are huddled up into a dense community and have no land, nor can they obtain it ... They are therefore solely dependent on the market for food, always unemployed when not at sea, liable to idle, improvident and intemperate habits, often starving and rarely above want. The materials for their boats bad, and as well as their clothes and bed clothes often in pawn.

The precarious existence of most of these fishermen completely unravelled during the Famine years from 1845 onwards. The severe weather conditions of 1845-6 prevented the fishermen from

106. Villagers planting seed potatoes at Skehacrine, Abbeyside c.1917.

107. A postcard of Home Rule Street c.1900. McGrath's Castle is in the background.

going to sea, particularly in boats which were in poor repair. Many fishermen had pawned their gear in the hope of recovering it the following year. Boats, oars, etc. were burned for fuel. As a result the supply of fish became scarce and prices went up, putting it out of reach of the poor. Other sea foods such as limpets and seaweed were accessible at low tide, but supplies did not last long with the large numbers picking them. By March 1847 the Waterford Freeman newspaper reported that 'people were picking Doolamaun [seaweed] on the beach in Dungarvan and eating it raw'.

The Famine caused much loss of life in Abbeyside and Dungarvan. The fever hospital at Strandside North accommodated 167 patients at its peak use in 1847. 125 of these patients were kept in temporary 'fever sheds'. Other

warehouse-type buildings around Abbeyside were used to house some of the almost 4,000 starving paupers of the locality. Carbery's Store on Strandside South had 550 inmates, primarily women but also some children. The nearby Galwey's Store held 200 children. By November 1846 an adult pauper's diet consisted of 10 ounces (245 g) of undigestible Indian meal mixed with treacle for both breakfast and dinner.

You cannot walk abroad for one moment that you are not appealed to by scores of poor creatures ... exhausted from hunger ... their tottering steps and emaciated countenances would at once convince you of the truth of their soul-sickening story. On Sunday last there were five funerals almost at the same time in Abbeyside ... from morning till night you are alarmed by the cries and miseries of hungry creatures.

Landlords exacerbated the disaster by evicting tenants who could not pay their rent. In 1848 'at Abbeyside more than 100 poor creatures had their homes levelled'. The ten houses were 'razed to the ground' so they could not be reoccupied by their starving tenants. The government response to the disaster was slow and insufficient. At the peak of the Famine in West Waterford, 4,000 starving paupers were housed in workhouses, 12,000 people were fed by soup kitchens, and thousands more were given low-paid work on famine relief programmes.

A crowd of labourers called to Father Jeremiah Halley's house in Bridge Street, Dungarvan appealing to him to obtain work for them. He asked them not to resort to violence or public disorder and stated that he would have work for them on the following day. On the following day he arranged for 400 men to be employed picking stones at Abbeyside beach at one shilling a day.

The Famine drove mass Irish emigration to England, America, Canada, Australia and elsewhere. Between 1851 and 1861 an average of 3,500 people emigrated to other countries from Co. Waterford each year. This increased to 8,200 people annually between 1881 and 1891.

As you would expect from a settlement built on the water's edge, Abbeyside is a village with a strong seafaring past. Generations of young Abbeyside men were drawn to a life at sea, and up until the recent past many households in the village included a sailor or fisherman. Some went on to achieve fame beyond the small village of their birth.

During World War II, on 27 March 1941, Captain Tom Donohue was in command of the SS Lady Belle when it was bombed and machine-gunned by the Luftwaffe while steaming from Dungarvan to Cardiff. Captain Donohue later served on board the SS Irish Oak, which was torpedoed by a German submarine on 15 May 1943. Surviving this, Captain Donohue went on to command the rescue for which he is still remembered today. On 29 December 1943 his ship, the MV Kerlogue, saved 168 injured and shipwrecked German sailors from the icy waters of the Bay of Biscay. Lieutenant Commander Joachim Quedenfeldt, the highest-ranking German rescued, later wrote of 'the little ship bravely moving through the enormous waves to pick up more and more of my comrades'. In December 1949 Captain Tom Donohue was laid to rest in Abbeyside graveyard within sight of the sea. His portrait still hangs in the Abbeyside Scout Den; in 1930 he and his wife generously donated the land on which the den was built.

108. Captain Tom Donohue, Sarsfield Street, Abbeyside c.1930.

Captain William Flynn from Abbeyside was a merchant seaman who was awarded three medals for the daring rescue of Dutch sailors and a European prince during a ferocious storm in the Bay of Biscay – one from the Queen of the Netherlands, one from the Dutch government and one from Lloyd's.

During the Irish War of Independence, Abbeyside was the location of one of the best-known events of the conflict in West Waterford. The Burgery Ambush was carried out by an active service unit (flying column) of the Irish Republican Army (IRA) on the night of 18-19 March 1921. Approximately seventeen British military personnel had gone in a lorry and car to Clonea to arrest IRA munitions expert John Murphy. The British forces, commanded by Captain D.V. Thomas and Lieutenant Griffith (or Griffiths – sources differ), comprised soldiers from the Buffs (Royal East Kent Regiment), Sergeant Michael Hickey of the Royal Irish Constabulary (RIC), and a group of Black and Tans. (The Black and Tans, officially the Royal Irish Constabulary Special Reserve, was a force of temporary RIC constables. The nickname arose from the colours of the uniforms they wore, a mix of British Army khaki and RIC rifle green.)

On the return journey with their captive along the main Waterford-Dungarvan road (now the N25) they ran into a hastily-prepared ambush. In overall command of the approximately twenty-man IRA unit was IRA GHQ officer George Plunkett, assisted by West Waterford Brigade Commandant Pax Whelan. The actual ambush, which could more accurately be described as a series of skirmishes, was prosecuted by a ten-man section under flying column commander George Lennon. Captain Thomas, Sergeant

109. IRA Volunteer Pat Keating, mortally wounded in the Burgery Ambush.

Hickey and two soldiers were captured. Hickey was executed as a police spy; he had previously been warned to leave his position in the police force. He knew the locality well and was acquainted with some of the IRA men since childhood. Captain Thomas and the two soldiers were released unharmed. In his report on the action, Thomas maintained he escaped his captors, but most evidence points to him having been released.

Burnings at Abbeyside, Dungarven. Strand Hotel, Apl. 15th 1921.

110. The Strand Hotel, Abbeyside, burned as a reprisal for the Burgery Ambush, 12 April 1921.

On the morning following the ambush a small group of the IRA men returned to the ambush site to recover weapons and ammunition. They stumbled into a strong detachment of British forces. In the ensuing shoot-out Pat Keating and Seán Fitzgerald were killed on the Republican side. Black and Tan Constable Sydney Redman was fatally wounded on the British side.

The immediate aftermath of the ambush saw the imposition of a rigorously-enforced curfew. In the days that followed, six or seven homes and business premises across Abbeyside and Dungarvan were destroyed. Up to twenty soldiers would descend on a premises with axes, sledges and crowbars to destroy all furniture, fixtures and fittings inside. Several women were physically assaulted during these reprisals.

On the night of 12 April 1921 Verey lights were shot into the air from the military base at Dungarvan Castle to illuminate Abbeyside. Soldiers descended on the village and burned the Strand Hotel at Strandside North and several houses along Sexton Street. Events such as these served to alienate the local population and only promoted the Republican cause. A monument to Pat Keating and Seán Fitzgerald is located at the approximate ambush site on the N25.

111. Opened in 1816, Devonshire Bridge connects Dungarvan to the village of Abbeyside.

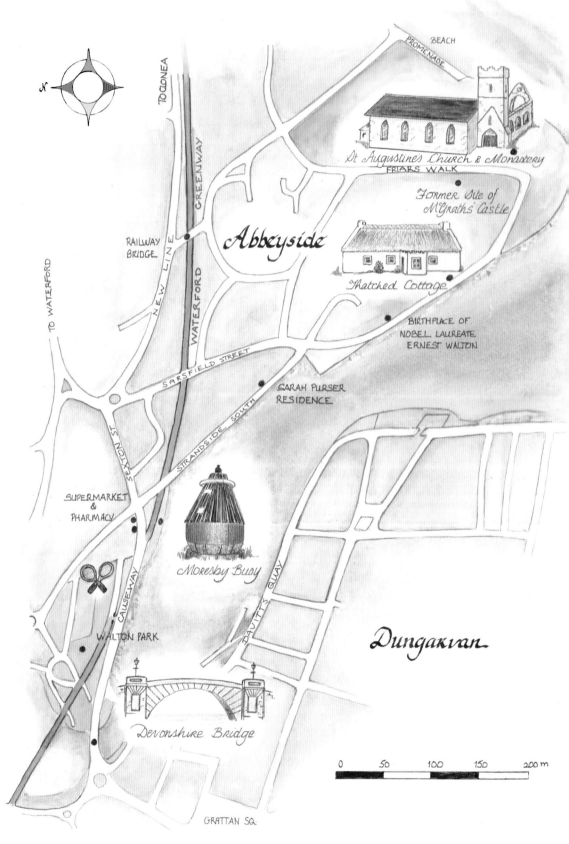

N

TO CLONEA

BEACH
PROMENADE

St Augustine's Church & Monastery
FRIARS WALK

Former Site of
McGraths' Castle

RAILWAY
BRIDGE

Abbeyside

Thatched Cottage

NEW LINE

WATERFORD GREENWAY

TO WATERFORD

SARSFIELD STREET

BIRTHPLACE OF
NOBEL LAUREATE
ERNEST WALTON

SARAH PURSER
RESIDENCE

STRANDSIDE SOUTH

SEXTON ST

SUPERMARKET
&
PHARMACY

Moresby Buoy

DAVITT'S QUAY

Dungarvan

CAUSEWAY

WALTON PARK

Devonshire Bridge

0   50   100   150   200 m

GRATTAN SQ.

112. Map of Abbeys.

Devonshire Bridge

Devonshire Bridge is not the first bridge to connect Dungarvan to the 'abbey side'. In 1214 the burgesses of Dungarvan (town or borough inhabitants with full rights of citizenship) received a royal grant of 'Breteuil', which meant that they had the same rights as the town of Breteuil in northern France. This allowed them to levy a crossing taxation for the maintenance of a Dungarvan bridge. The exact location of this early bridge is unknown – it may have been at Ballyneety Bridge, 2 km north of Dungarvan along the Colligan estuary.

The current bridge which connects the town of Dungarvan to the village of Abbeyside is the elegant Devonshire Bridge. It spans the River Colligan as it flows into Dungarvan Bay. The bridge was commissioned by William Cavendish, 5th Duke of Devonshire, as part of the early 19th-century reconstruction of Dungarvan town centre. Costing £5,000 to build, this single-span bridge finally opened in 1816. Designed by William Atkinson, and built with rusticated sandstone imported from Runcorn in Cheshire, it remains an impressive local landmark with commanding views over Dungarvan harbour. The bridge, as originally planned, would have had multiple spans stretching across the harbour, but the cost of such a grand scheme proved prohibitive. It was decided to reduce construction costs by building a causeway (a road atop an embankment of stone and soil) across Dungarvan Bay to connect to the much-shortened bridge.

Devonshire Bridge and the connecting Causeway (as it is still known locally) substantially enhanced the transport infrastructure of Dungarvan. Historically, crossing from Abbeyside to Dungarvan was via ferry, if you had money to pay the ferryman. Alternatively, you could wait for low tide and wade across. In 1842 this scene was memorably described by the novelist William Makepeace Thackeray for his travel guide, *The Irish Sketch Book*: 'this wide estuary was called "Dungarvan Prospect" because the ladies of the country, walking over the river at low water took off their shoes and stockings (such as had them) and tucking up their clothes, exhibited – what I have never seen, and cannot therefore be expected to describe'.

Moresby Buoy

The start of the Greenway in Abbeyside is marked by the *Moresby* buoy, a memorial to both the town's seafaring tradition and an unfortunate tragedy. This Wigham lighted buoy originally marked the location in Dungarvan Bay where the sailing ship Moresby sank on Christmas Eve 1895. The *Moresby* left Cardiff on 21 December 1895 carrying a cargo of 1,778 tons of coal and bound for Pisagua in Chile. There was a crew of twenty-three including the captain, Caleb Francis Coomber. The captain's wife Edith Isabella (29) and their daughter Ivy (2¼) were also aboard.

At 2.30 p.m. on 23 December, the keeper of Ballinacourty Lighthouse saw the *Moresby* in distress. The ship dropped anchor about three-quarters of a mile from the lighthouse. At 4.00 p.m. the Ballinacourty lifeboat rowed out to the ship to ascertain if the crew wished to be taken off, but none of them did. The weather deteriorated overnight and the *Moresby* sent out distress signals. About

113. *The volunteer lifeboat crew involved in the Moresby rescue on Christmas Eve 1895.*

4.30 a.m. on 24 December the anchor broke and the ship capsized. By 11.00 a.m. the masts had dropped closer to the water and as the crew saw no sign of a lifeboat coming to their rescue they decided to swim for shore. The original lifeboat crew had refused to put to sea again. A volunteer lifeboat crew from Dungarvan was hastily assembled and set out to rescue the remaining crew, most of whom were in the sea.

Sixteen-year-old ship's apprentice Henry Blount recalled the rescue:

I had been in the water nearly an half an hour when I saw the lifeboat coming towards me ... I was not more than 300 or 400 yards from the ship when I was dragged into the lifeboat thoroughly exhausted ...

Three Russian Finns and a Scotchman were afterwards picked up. Michie was also taken in, but he appeared to be dead, as he never revived. Ten or twenty minutes later Barker was likewise rescued from the sea ... but died directly we reached shore...

When we landed, I was carried to the Coastguard station ... I was provided with warm clothing ... and was shortly afterwards taken to Dungarvan Hospital, where I remained until the morning after Christmas Day. I was then fetched to identify the bodies which had been washed up.

Gregory's body was brought in by the tide on Friday, seven or eight miles from Dungarvan ... Barker was buried on Friday, and Gregory on Saturday, in the Protestant Churchyard at Dungarvan ... When I left on Saturday, part of the hull and one of the masts was all that could be seen of the 'Moresby'. The bodies of the Captain, his wife and child were washed ashore, and were all buried in one grave. The baby was washed ashore just as we were leaving Dungarvan on Saturday.

Twenty out of the twenty-five crew and passengers were drowned. Most of those drowned in the disaster were buried in St Mary's Church of Ireland cemetery, the majority in a mass grave.

Close to the *Moresby* buoy memorial is a bench known as the 'Poor Man's Seat'. Whilst the seat has been replaced many times, the location is still a traditional meeting point for locals, much as it was for sailors of past generations.

Walton Causeway Park

At the very start (or end) of the Greenway in Dungarvan is Walton Causeway Park, named after the experimental physicist and Nobel Prize winner, Professor Ernest T. S. Walton (1903-1995). Walton was born in the now demolished Epworth Cottage at Strandside South, Abbeyside in October 1903, the son of the local Methodist minister, John Arthur Walton. His mother was Ann Elizabeth Sinton from Tandragee, Co. Armagh. On 14 April 1932 at Cambridge University's Cavendish Laboratory, Walton split the atom with John Cockcroft. In recognition of this work they shared the Nobel Prize for Physics in 1951. Ernest Walton is one of only two Irish scientists to ever receive this honour. A plaque marking Walton's birthplace was erected on the site of his childhood home by the National Committee for Science and Engineering Commemorative Plaques. Built entirely on reclaimed land, this park was under water until the 1980s. The pedestrian footbridge in the park is the old railway bridge across the River Colligan.

Sarah Purser (1848-1943)

Portrait painter, stained glass artist and pioneering female arts administrator, Sarah Purser was born on 22 March 1848 in Kingstown (now Dún Laoghaire), a coastal town south of Dublin. Her father Benjamin Purser, a flour miller and brewer, and his wife Ann Mallet moved their family to Abbeyside soon after Sarah's birth. It became her home for the next twenty-five years. A plaque erected at Strandside South marks the location of the first home of the Purser family in the locality. The family later moved to a house called the Hermitage, elsewhere in Abbeyside. Purser left Dungarvan in the summer of 1873 to make her living as a painter and settled in Dublin. Working as a portraitist, she was very successful in obtaining commissions, famously commenting, 'I went through the British aristocracy like the measles'. Her oil on canvas, 'A double portrait of Constance and Eva Gore-Booth as young girls in a woodland setting', sold at auction for €239,000 in 2003.

In 1903 Purser founded An Túr Gloine (Irish for the Glass Tower), the first Irish stained glass studio of its kind. She was instrumental in drawing the attention of the art world to the works of John Butler Yeats and Nathaniel Hone. She was involved in the setting up of the Hugh Lane Municipal Gallery, the foremost public collection of contemporary art in Ireland. In 1914 she became the second woman to sit on the Board of Governors and Guardians of the National Gallery of Ireland. In 1924 she became the first female member of the Royal Hibernian Academy.

114. A train passing through the Causeway level crossing, Abbeyside 1967.
(Photo © Michael J. Walsh; reproduced courtesy of The Irish Railway Record Society)

115. *The Hermitage, Abbeyside c.1910, childhood home of the artist Sarah Purser.*

116. *A single-storey thatched cottage, Strandside South, Abbeyside, built c.1780-1800.*

Thatched cottage, Strandside South

Thatch was once a common choice for roofing and thatched cottages dotted the Irish landscape. Maintenance costs and construction trends mean that only 2,500 thatched cottages remain in Ireland today. The last remaining example in the village of Abbeyside is at Strandside South. This detached four-bay single-storey thatched cottage was built between 1780 and 1820 and retains some of its early windows. It was extended c.1950. The pitched roof has a reed thatch in the English style with rope work to the ridge, rendered squat chimney stacks and rendered coping. The walls are made of either mud or stone rubble with a painted render. A roof made from reed thatch typically lasts between forty to fifty years, but the roof ridge normally has to be replaced roughly every eight years or so.

McGrath's Castle

No trace now remains above ground of this building but for over 500 years McGrath's Castle was an Abbeyside landmark. This tower house (a fortified medieval residence) associated with the O'Brien and McGrath families stood at Friar's Walk, opposite the Augustinian abbey (the current Abbeyside parish church). The building was one of the first sights seen by sailors as they approached Dungarvan harbour. Such was the castle's prominence that it represents the village of Abbeyside on the Dungarvan town coat of arms, redesigned by William Williams in 1863. The earliest Gaelic name for Abbeyside is Dún na Mainistreach or fort of the monastery. It is possible that the settlement predates the Anglo-Norman arrival in the 13th century.

117. The southern facade of McGrath's Castle, Friars Walk, Abbeyside c.1900.

The O'Brien clan were one of the prominent Déise (Waterford) tribes. Their allies the McGraths are believed to have built this tower house in the early 15th century, possibly on the site of an earlier settlement. McGrath's Castle stood on one acre of land and comprised six stories supported by stone vaults. A description from 1841 gives us a good idea of the building's size: 'It is a lofty square building measuring on the outside 38 feet from east to west and 31 feet 6 inches from north to south and its walls are well grouted and eight feet in thickness ... not less than 90 feet in height'.

The McGraths were protectors and patrons of the neighbouring Augustinian abbey. Until the 17th century they controlled lands stretching from Abbeyside to Kilgobinet and on to the Comeragh Mountains. The family's local dominance came to an end with the victory of the Parliamentarian army under Oliver Cromwell during the Irish Confederate Wars (1641-53). The castle featured prominently in these wars. It was of strategic importance to the defence of Dungarvan and changed hands on several occasions. Armies seeking to bombard and lay siege to the town from Abbeyside were threatened to their rear and flanks by McGrath's Castle.

Over time the tower house fell into disrepair and it partially collapsed in 1916. In the 1960s the remaining walls of the castle were finally demolished as they were unsafe. Today a plaque erected by the McGrath clan marks the location where the castle once stood overlooking Dungarvan Bay. A modern housing estate built on the site was named Castle Keep as an acknowledgement of the site's history.

St Augustine's Priory

The village of Abbeyside derives its name from St Augustine's Priory. A priory in simple terms is a small abbey managed by a prior. Technically, a minimum of twelve monks were required to form an abbey. The building has been described as a church of national significance, on account of the continuation of a long-standing ecclesiastical presence on site. The current parish church incorporates the fabric of a much earlier medieval Augustinian priory, built c.1290. The bell tower, dating from c.1450, gave the ruins the local name of 'the Clogchas', a name derived from the old Irish for belfry (bell tower). The priory was founded by the Augustinian order, who came from Clare Priory in Suffolk, England. They were invited over by their patron Thomas FitzGerald. FitzGerald was appointed Justiciar of Ireland in 1295 by King Edward I of England. This position was roughly equivalent to that of a modern prime minister. Thomas FitzGerald had an unusual nickname. Legend has him being snatched from his cradle by an ape when he was a child. Fortunately for the future foundation of Abbeyside he was returned safely to his cot by the ape. Ever after this incident Thomas was nicknamed Tomás an Apa or Thomas Simiacus.

A story about the arrival of the Augustinians tells of how they were undecided where to land when they sailed into Dungarvan Bay. After praying for guidance, they launched a small raft with a statue of St Augustine on it. Where the raft came ashore is where they decided to build their abbey.

The original building was constructed with traditional rubble walls. These are

3 WALLS of THE OLD CASTLE ABBEYSIDE COLLAPSED ON JAN. 18th. 1916. (KEOXAM.)

118. *The ruins of McGrath's Castle, Abbeyside after it collapsed on 18 January 1916.*

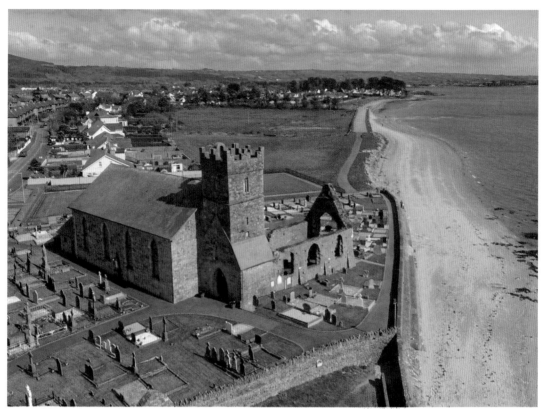

119. Abbeyside church incorporates the remains of an Augustinian priory, built c.1290.

built using a variety of building stones and a lime mortar. The lime is mixed with sand and this makes for a strong mortar. This method of construction is the same as that used in constructing the thatched cottages which dotted the landscape once upon a time. The walls, both inside and out, were treated to several coats of whitewash, a solution of lime and water used for painting walls white. In other Irish monasteries the whitewashed interiors were decorated with paintings of parables and scenes from the Bible. It is likely that the priory at Abbeyside was decorated in a similar fashion. These illustrations were helpful teaching aids and helped illustrate sermons delivered at Mass.

The current dull appearance of the priory ruin is a far cry from the building's whitewashed heyday. The shining white monastery acted as a beacon for ships approaching Dungarvan. Sailors leaving Dungarvan harbour lowered their sails three times as they passed the Abbey. This practice was common well into the 19th century.

The life of an Augustinian monk was not an easy one. Following the rules laid down by St Augustine involved a life of poverty, obedience, chastity, detachment from the world, fasting and abstinence, care of the sick, silence and reading during meals. At their 14th-century peak, the Augustinian order had over 800 friars across England and Ireland.

The monastic life was generally one of hard physical work, scholarship and prayer. The monastery at Abbeyside would have been much more than a place of prayer – it was also a place of work, and of learning. The monks grew their own food, tended herds of animals, and did all their own building. During the medieval period, monasteries were practically the only repositories of scholarship and learning. As a general rule, monks were by far the best-educated members of society – indeed, in a small community like Abbeyside, they were often the only educated members of society. Our priory makes occasional appearances in the historical record. In 1312 the prior, Roger, was sued by Adam Brown who had given a bequest of seven acres of land to the abbey in return for Masses being celebrated for his soul. He was not best pleased when the land was sold on to John Tyrell against his wishes. Thomas McGrath, who was prior in 1488, was probably a member of the McGrath family who controlled the nearby castle.

The end of this first phase of Christian occupation on the site came with the the Dissolution of the Monasteries in 1541. Sometimes referred to as the Suppression of the Monasteries, this was a set of anti-Catholic administrative and legal processes carried out between 1536 and 1541. King Henry VIII disbanded Roman Catholic monasteries, priories and convents across England, Wales and Ireland, appropriated their income and disposed of their assets. This was a catastrophe for monastic life and the monastery at Abbeyside was not to be spared. When the monastery was dissolved in 1541 the records show that it functioned as the local parish church. The monastic buildings on the two-acre site were deemed to be suitable for farming use. The holdings of the abbey included 165 acres, four dwelling-houses with adjacent buildings, thirty-eight small homes with gardens, and a subsidiary farm known as a camera. This is the earliest known description of the village of Abbeyside.

The present church was built in 1832. By the 1850s, parish priest Fr Thomas O'Meara decided to take steps to protect the abbey tower and felt he had to renovate the church due to the dilapidated condition it was in. He raised funds from parishioners to restore the church to something approaching a good state of repair. The generosity of the parishioners was remarkable considering that the fundraising took place towards the end of the Famine period. The marble altar was purchased at a cost of £150, a considerable sum of money at that time. The consecration of the restored church took place on 26 September 1858.

Grave markers

The majority of the cut-stone grave markers in the graveyard attached to the church date from around 1830 to the present day. A notable exception is the tomb of Donal McGrath. His limestone grave slab, dated 1470, is set into the ground underneath the archway entrance to the Clogchas. Wandering around the cemetery you will see the family names associated with life in the village over the past 200 years. A few grave markers are of particular interest.

Commander Eugene Sarsfield (1902-1943)

Inside the Clogchas can be found a simple marker to the Sarsfield family. Patrick Sarsfield was born at Abbeyside in 1865 and emigrated to America in 1890.

120. Two ships moored at the graving bank beside the Causeway, Abbeyside c.1910.

His son Eugene Sylvester Sarsfield was born in 1902. A career naval officer, he distinguished himself in combat during World War II. He was executive officer and navigator of USS *Kearny* when the destroyer was torpedoed off Iceland on 17 October 1941. He was commended by the Secretary of the US Navy, Frank Knox, for 'leadership, personal courage and ingenuity in solving the many problems arising under adverse conditions' after this action. On 6 May 1943, his ship USS *Maddox* attacked and sank an enemy submarine whilst providing an escort for an Atlantic convoy. He was awarded the Legion of Merit for exceptionally meritorious conduct.

On 10 July 1943 USS *Maddox* was

supporting the invasion of Sicily when the destroyer was struck by a bomb from a German Ju 88 bomber. Sarsfield remained on board to supervise the evacuation of the rapidly sinking ship. He helped save the lives of nine officers and sixty-five men of the 284 crew. Sarsfield was cited for extraordinary heroism and was posthumously awarded the United States military's second-highest decoration, the Navy Cross. The destroyer USS *Sarsfield* (DD-837), launched on 27 May 1945, was named in his honour. Sarsfield Playground in Brooklyn, New York was also named after him.

Pádraig Ó Dálaigh (1873-1932), Secretary of the Gaelic League

To the left as you enter Abbeyside graveyard a Celtic cross marks the grave of Irish-language activist, poet and publisher, Pádraig Ó Dálaigh. Born Patrick Daly to John and Mary Daly of the Burgery, Abbeyside, Ó Dálaigh played a major role in the Gaelic revival movement spearheaded by the Gaelic League. Founded in 1893, with the aim of restoring the rapidly declining Irish language, the League felt that language was central to maintaining an Irish identity. It ran Irish language classes countrywide, published many new texts in the native language, and standardised the writing of Irish.

From an early age Ó Dálaigh had a great interest in Irish culture, with a particular love of the Irish language. He organised several local branches of the Gaelic League, before assuming the role of general secretary for the national organisation in Dublin. For nineteen years he was at the forefront of all of the association's work. A contemporary left this wonderful pen portrait of him:

[H]*e has repeatedly performed the following things simultaneously: written letters, spoken in Irish and English, checked branch reports, read press notices – and smiled ... When anyone with a grievance comes in and threatens to wreck the movement he is folded in the magic of the Secretary's smile and his anger is put to sleep...*

As the Gaelic League became more of a political movement, Ó Dálaigh decided to leave to become a director of the Educational Book Company of Ireland and the Talbot Press. For twenty years he oversaw the editing and publication of Ireland's primary school books. He is buried with his sister Cáit Walsh.

Ballinacourty

Neighbouring the village of Abbeyside, on the northern headland that shelters Dungarvan Bay, is the townland of Ballinacourty. The placename Ballinacourty – Baile na Cúirte, or town of the manor house – refers to the home of the Wyse family who lived here from the early 17th century. In 1641 an attempted coup d'état by Irish Catholic gentry occurred. They tried to seize control of the English administration in Ireland to force concessions for Catholics. After the 1641 rebellion, Andrew Wyse decided to leave Ballinacourty and move to Waterford city but the family retained the estate, leasing it to various tenants well into the 19th century. The Wyse family were prominent in the life of Waterford city and Sir Thomas Wyse (1791-1862) married Laetitia Bonaparte, the niece of French emperor Napoleon Bonaparte. Ballinacourty House was occupied from about 1700 by the Longan family who originally came from Limerick, where a number of them were mayors of the city from the 13th century. The house no longer exists and the grounds are now part of a golf course.

The official name is Ballynacourty but most locals use the 'Ballinacourty' spelling. Previous spellings include Ballynecowrty (1558), Ballenecourtie (1578), Ballinicourt (1603), Ballynacoorty (1657) Ballycourty (1659) and finally Ballinacourty (1841). However you spell it, you will find some of the tastiest 'spuds' in Ireland here: the area is famous for producing the best early potatoes.

121. Ballinacourty village with Elsted's public house in the foreground c.1900.

In the early 20th century the name of the local potato growing co-operative was the Dungarvan and Ballinacourty Potato Growers' Association. The name reflected the pre-eminent position of the Ballinacourty potato crop.

Ballinacourty is home to the Gold Coast Road and a modern hotel of the same name. The name comes from a 19th-century thatched public house that once stood where the Gold Coast Hotel is now. The public house was renamed the Gold Coast in the 1950s by owner John Elsted and the name stuck to the locality. The Ballinacourty Coastguard Station stood in what is now the Gold Coast Golf Club. Serving as a coastguard station since at least 1845, it was rebuilt in 1881. It featured prominently in many rescues.

On 19 February 1861 the coastguards went to aid the brigantine Susan; they were rewarded for their bravery with two RNLI silver medals. During the Irish War of Independence the coastguards were an important part of the British forces controlling the area. On the night of 9 August 1922, at the height of the Irish Civil War, Republicans burned the station to the ground to deny the building to the National Army. The fuel that was used for the burning was taken from the nearby Ballinacourty Lighthouse. (The 13m high lighthouse was established on 1 July 1858.) The coastguard station was renovated and became the clubhouse of Dungarvan Golf Club in 1939. On 19 September 1989 the former coastguard building went on fire for a second and final time. This time it did not rise like a phoenix from the ashes, and the building had to be demolished.

Opposite the entrance to the picturesque Ballinacourty Lighthouse is Kilgrovan, a townland of considerable archaeological significance. Derived from the Irish Cill Ghrúbhán, church of Grúbhán, no trace of this church remains. Kilgrovan had a substantial early ecclesiastical bivallate (twin-walled) enclosure which was levelled in the 1960s. Five ogham stones were discovered in this townland by William Williams in 1857. The stones may have been located in various parts of the surrounding area and gathered to one location. The stones were incorporated into field boundaries until the historian Canon Power arranged for them to be transported to the Cistercian abbey at Mount Melleray in 1900. They can be viewed there to this day. A further two ogham stones were discovered in the 1960s and these are now in the National Museum of Ireland. Bii ware (sherds of a late Roman amphora) were found at Kilgrovan dating to the late 5th and early 6th centuries. Amphorae were often used to contain or transport wine or olive oil.

122. Ballinacourty Lighthouse.

Clonea

Clonea is best known for the 3 km long Clonea Strand, located approximately 5 km outside Dungarvan. Very popular with tourists, it is a long, wide sandy beach with fantastic views and scenic walks.

Clonea is derived from the Irish Cluain Fhia, meaning meadow of the deer. Today, one would have to do some searching to find a deer at Clonea.

A prominent landmark on the coastline for two centuries was Clonea Castle which was destroyed during a winter storm in the early 1990s. It was built in the 18th century as a folly (an ornamental building with no practical purpose) in imitation of a medieval castle by Arthur MccGwire who was the local landlord. He lived in the nearby Clonea House which still survives today and which can be seen from the Greenway. Both structures were built near the cliff edge to take advantage of the magnificent sea views. Walter MccGwire had been a judge in India where he is said to have had an Indian wife. On his retirement in 1800, he returned to the family home at Clonea bringing his Indian *ayah* (nursemaid or nanny) with him. His brother Richard, a student at Trinity College, took part in a celebrated hot-air-balloon trip in Dublin in 1785 for which he was given a silver medal by Trinity and a knighthood by the Viceroy (the representative of the King in Ireland).

Another substantial historical landmark that remains at Clonea is the ruin of the old church or priory with adjacent graveyard. It stands to the rear of a private holding and is not accessible to visitors. It was a very early centre of worship and is believed to predate St Patrick. Very little now remains of the original structure, but some traces of primitive masonry can still be seen.

123. *The Ocean View Hotel and tennis courts, Clonea c.1940.*

124. The Cunnigar.

STRADBALLY

A picturesque 18th-century village with medieval roots.

*I*n 1215, King John granted the custody of the counties of Waterford and Desmond (most of Cork and Kerry) to Thomas fitz Anthony. This was a reward for fitz Anthony's support for the king in fighting rebel barons in England at the time. Thomas fitz Anthony seems to have founded the medieval town of Stradbally, which was situated at the centre of his lordship (he also founded Thomastown in Co. Kilkenny). The name Stradbally is derived from the Irish *sráidbhaile*, meaning village (literally street-town), and this is probably a reference to the medieval settlement. Thomas fitz Anthony died in 1226 or 1227 and the lordship subsequently passed to one of his sons-in-law, Thomas de Dene. When *his* son Reginald died in 1302, he held a quarter of the town of Stradbally from the king. Stradbally subsequently passed to a branch of the FitzGeralds,

Earls of Desmond, who held it until the early eighteenth century. In 1300, when King Edward I levied his Irish domains to finance his war against Scotland, Stradbally was one of five towns in the county to be assessed for special payments. We also know that Stradbally had a mill – there are references to it in 1298 and 1336 – but we do not know its location. All this suggests that Stradbally was an important medieval town. All that remains of medieval Stradbally, however, is its church; it is not known what became of the rest of the town. In 1654 the Civil Survey described Stradbally as 'a County Towne with a greate many howses', which suggests that the medieval settlement had survived in some form up until then.

The present village of Stradbally dates from around the end of the eighteenth century, and was built by the Uniacke family of Woodhouse, who owned the

Stradbally Village — 19009.

202. A colour postcard of Stradbally village, c.1900.

village and most of the surrounding district. At the centre of the village is a market square surrounded by terraces of two-storey houses and businesses. The three-storey building which dominates the east side of the square is a former police barracks, and is probably slightly older than the buildings around it. Set back from the square is the Old Rectory, home of successive Church of Ireland incumbents until 1939. It was bought by the Sisters of Mercy in 1943. In 1970, in collaboration with the then rector, Canon David Clarke, the sisters hosted Ireland's first ever ecumenical clerical retreat in the house.

Stradbally has two churches. St James' Church of Ireland church is located at the top of Church Lane, just behind the ruined medieval church. Work on this church began with the appointment of John Devereux as Vicar of Stradbally in 1798. The main body of the church was completed in 1802, with the addition of a tower four years later. The tower was originally topped with a spire, but this was removed in 1876 when the chancel was added. The church also had a gallery, accessed from the first floor of the belfry (bell tower), but this is also long since gone. The church was dedicated to St James in 1970. It is typical of the numerous Church of Ireland churches built by the Board of First Fruits in the late eighteenth and early nineteenth centuries. The Board was an institution of the Church of Ireland that was established in 1711 by Queen Anne to build and improve churches in Ireland. Holy Cross Catholic church is located a short distance outside the village. A Woodhouse estate map from 1819 shows a church just south of where the present church now stands. The present

church, a large, single-cell, barn-type structure, was built in 1834. Stained glass windows were added in 1868, followed by an imposing tower in 1870 and an apse in 1873. These additions were largely funded by the Barron family.

The Sisters of Mercy came to Stradbally in 1875 at the invitation of the parish priest, Fr Thomas Casey. Initially they lived in Myrtle Lodge (adjacent to the Old Rectory, and which itself had served as a rectory earlier in the century), then in 1883 they moved into what had been Hannigan's Hotel in the square (now Whelan's pub). Some visitors to the village were unaware of the building's

203. Canon F.H. Burkitt, Rector of Stradbally 1888-1939, on his penny-farthing, June 1936.

204. The Square, Stradbally, in the late 1920s.

new role, and one anecdote tells of how an inebriated woman arrived into the hall one evening and requested a half glass, only to be rapidly sobered up by the sight of the nuns! When Fr Casey died in 1885, the sisters moved into the former parochial house behind Holy Cross Church, renaming it Mount St Joseph's. They also built a school in the grounds, which opened in 1890. In addition to this the sisters established a small linen industry to give employment to local girls. The industry was successful and lasted for over thirty years, but mass production and cheap imports led to its closure in 1925. Dwindling vocations led to the convent's closure in 1988.

The school established by the sisters was not the only one in the village. A Church of Ireland primary school was built by Uniacke family of Woodhouse around the beginning of the nineteenth century, opposite the Church of Ireland church. In 1819, the school was kept by the curate, who taught 'English, Greek and Latin, at £30 per annum for boarders, and four guineas for day boys'. The school has opened and shut several times, depending on numbers, but it continues in use to this day as St James' National School. In 1806, local Catholic landowner Pierce Barron opened a school 'for the gratuitous education of the poor of the parish'. The building was divided in two

205. Holy Cross Catholic church c.1910.

– boys were taught at one end and girls at the other. The building functioned as a boys' school until 1966 when the new boys' school opened nearby. The Barron School was repurposed as a community hall, and has been extensively restored in recent years.

Stradbally GAA Club was founded in 1886. Gaelic football has always been the dominant sport in the parish, with the Stradbally team winning five-in-a-row senior county football titles from 1940 to 1944 and again from 2001 to 2005. Gaelic games were played in a variety of locations in the district, before the club acquired a permanent pitch in the early 1970s. A clubhouse was built in 1979. The GAA ground is named after local priest Fr Pat Cummins, who trained the Stradbally team in the early 1940s. The important role of Gaelic games in the parish is also evidenced by the handball alley on the Chapel Road, built in 1934.

Stradbally today is an attractive, well-kept village, the recipient of numerous Tidy Towns awards.

206. Pierce Barron of Faha (c.1726-1810), who founded the Barron School.

207. Stradbally village c.1973.

N

STRADBALLY COVE

Stradbally

Woodhouse
Estate

R675

DURROW
VIADUCT

Durrow

GREENWAY

DURROW
TUNNEL

Ballyvoile

BALLYVOILE
VIADUCT

0 100 200 300 400 500 600 700

208. Map of Stradb

Medieval church

Stradbally's ruined medieval church is situated beside the present Church of Ireland church. A large building, it comprises three sections – the nave, the chancel and the tower. The oldest (c.1215) and largest part of the church is the nave, rectangular in shape and over 17 metres long. It consists of two doorways, one each in the north and south walls. Either side of the north doorway are draw-bar sockets, for securing the door on the inside; in times of danger, the bar was drawn across and reinforced the door. Just inside the south doorway is a stoup or font for holy water, carved out of a single block of sandstone. The west gable was once surmounted by a bell-cot (a small shelter for the church bell), which was still there when John O'Donovan from the Ordnance Survey visited in 1841. This has now gone, but the remains of a small window can still be seen. Originally there would have been an arch connecting the nave with the chancel, but this is also now gone. The present chancel is a post-medieval rebuild. In the sanctuary, against the east gable, is the burial place of the Powers of Ballyvoile – the inscription on the gravestone outlines their genealogy in detail, although doubt has been cast on elements of it.

The tower probably dates from the thirteenth or fourteenth century, and consisted of three storeys. What now remains of the tower is the north half; the south half may have collapsed into the original chancel, necessitating the reconstruction of same. It is not quite clear how one actually entered the tower, but possibly there was a doorway in the north wall of the chancel. In the surviving north portion of the tower are the remains of a spiral staircase and a garderobe or toilet. The tower probably served as a residence for the priest.

Perhaps due to its spacious interior, the church has often been mistaken for an Augustinian abbey. This belief probably stems from the fact that for over 300 years, the church was in the possession of the Augustinian Priory of Inistioge which, like Stradbally, was founded by Thomas fitz Anthony. In 1540, at the height of the Reformation, the church and rectory of Stradbally were taken over by the Crown, and came under the control of the Bishop of Lismore. We do not know precisely how long the church remained open after this. In 1615 it was described as being in a dilapidated state. The oldest dated gravestone is that of Michael Martin who died in 1717, which suggests that the church was almost certainly in ruins by that time. The gravestone is adorned with a skull and crossbones, a common symbol of mortality at the time.

The most unusual feature of the ruined church is not the church itself but an inscribed gravestone which lies prone in the corner of the nave. Around the edge of the stone is an inscription, the surviving portion of which reads: 'YSABELLA GAL… JACET PLNI'. The top of the stone is covered in a variety of symbols, most of which seem to have some Christian significance, including the lily (symbolising the Resurrection) and the all-seeing eye, though this is a matter of interpretation. The stone is a mystery. We do not know how it ended up in the church – it probably dates from around 1600, when the church was quite possibly still in use. We do not know who Ysabella was either. It has been speculated that she was a Galvin or

209. St James' Church of Ireland church (built 1802) and the ruined medieval church (c.1215).

Galwey, both of which are local names. Indeed, one nineteenth-century scholar thought that the stone had nothing to do with anyone named Ysabella, and suggested - improbably - that if the inscription was complete, it would read: 'Beneath this altar lie the remains of Blessed Paulinus'.

Stradbally Cove

Stradbally Cove, a sheltered sandy beach, is situated just down the hill from the village. Early maps refer to it as 'Blind Cove'. The cove is unusual in that it is surrounded by mature trees. In 1742, Maurice Uniacke of Woodhouse obtained a premium for having planted 152,640 trees around his estate, and it is thought that the trees either side of the cove were among this number. Set into the hill at the back of the cove is a limekiln, built around 1800. Lime was shipped to the cove then burned in the kiln for use as fertiliser and for painting houses. There was also a coal yard nearby - coal was brought up the River Tay from a boat anchored at Pláicín Rock at the entrance to the cove. Colonel George John Beresford of Woodhouse built a boathouse at the cove in 1860 which he let to the local Coastguard for the sum of £5 per annum during his lifetime. (The Coastguard lived in a terrace of houses on High Street in the village.)

Woodhouse

The history of Woodhouse dates back to the end of the thirteenth century, when Thomas An Apa FitzGerald bequeathed Tigh na Coille (house in the woods) to his younger son Sir Thomas of Athasell. Throughout the tumultuous medieval

210. Picnicking at Stradbally Cove c.1900.

period and up until 1724 this large demesne along with the village of Stradbally belonged to the FitzGerald family. During the Munster Plantation Woodhouse was rented to an English undertaker, James Wallis. Undertakers were wealthy colonists who 'undertook' to import tenants from England to work their new lands in Ireland. These English undertakers were obliged to develop new towns and provide for the defence of planted districts from attack. Wallis invested heavily in the estate, building a 'fine stone house' and establishing a good working farm, before the bloody rebellion of 1641 when he was ousted from the property. The rebellion was an attempted coup d'état by Irish Catholic gentry, who tried to seize control of the English administration in Ireland to force concessions for Catholics. The sale of the property in 1724 to the prominent Uniacke family of Youghal and Mount Uniacke meant many architectural and administrative changes to Woodhouse. However, owing to the tragic fates of the children of the family, the Uniackes only held Woodhouse for 120 years. In 1844 the last Uniacke heiress, Frances Constantia, married George John Beresford, grandson of famous Irish statesman John Beresford and great-nephew of the 1st Marquess of Waterford. This marriage created one of many connections with Curraghmore which is still the seat of the Marquess of Waterford. Despite the couple having many children, none of these children had any issue of their own. In 1934, Lady Emily Hodson (nee Beresford) bequeathed Woodhouse to her Curraghmore relative, Lord Hugh Beresford (1908-41). Lord Hugh introduced many changes to the house but he was not destined to live there for long. On 23 May 1941 he was killed during the Battle of Crete while Lieutenant Commander on HMS *Kelly*. Lord Hugh's older brother Lord

211. View of Woodhouse, Stradbally c.1953.

212. Stradbally Cove.

William (1905-73) inherited Woodhouse and ran it to the best of his ability as a very successful farm. However, his failing health, seriously jeopardised during the Second World War, did not permit him to continue his work and in 1971 Woodhouse was sold outside of the family. Over the subsequent forty years it changed hands several times (singer Michael Jackson was interested in buying it at one stage) until in 2012 the house and 500 acres were bought by Jim and Sally Thompson. The couple went to an enormous effort to renovate Woodhouse and thanks to them it is now enjoying a new lease of life.

In 2017, the Woodhouse Museum was opened in what were formerly the stables. The museum aims to commemorate the history of the house and the people who lived and worked in it over the past 800 years in a comprehensive way. It is also hoped that the museum will help to collect the oral history of the area as well as documents of local interest.

Cloch Labhrais

On the bank of Deehal stream, about a mile from Durrow Station, stands Cloch Labhrais, the Speaking Stone. Cloch Labhrais is a large glacial boulder, split evenly in two. There are many versions of the legend associated with the stone. Sir Richard Cox recorded one version in the 1680s. According to Cox, the stone was formerly regarded as an oracle, and persons charged with crimes would go to the stone, which would pronounce them guilty or innocent as the case was. On one occasion a woman accused of adultery was summoned to appear before the stone. However, she arranged for the man with whom she was having the affair to impersonate a poor hermit and to be ready at the ford in the stream where the stone is situated. When she arrived, he asked her to carry him over the stream, which she did. She then swore on the stone 'that no body had ever been upon her', except of course her husband and the hermit. *Bíonn an fhírinne féin searbh*, said Cloch Labhrais,

213. Cloch Labhrais, mid-19th-century line drawing by George Victor Du Noyer.

meaning 'the truth itself is bitter', and it promptly split in two.

It is often said that Cloch Labhrais never spoke again after that. However, a more recent legend tells of how some local boys were poaching salmon at the stream one night when the police came on the scene, and in order to save the boys from being captured the stone broke its silence and told them which escape route to take. Not only that, but the stone apparently 'shook with laughter' when the poachers got away!

The importance of Cloch Labhrais as a landmark is evidenced by its appearance on early maps of the county. *Bíonn an fhírinne searbh* is a phrase still current in modern Irish.

Durrow viaduct and Durrow House

The viaduct at Durrow is one of three along the Greenway. Unlike the other two (at Ballyvoile and Kilmacthomas), the viaduct at Durrow is a viaduct over a bridge over a river. An impressive limestone structure with seven arches,

214. Durrow viaduct.

it was completed by 1878. The stone for the viaduct came from the Ballyvoile tunnel. It is said that the stones in the piers – weighing up to three tons – were put in place by sliding them down on long planks. Visible from the viaduct is Durrow House, birthplace of Irish language scholar Philip Barron (c.1801-44). Barron played an active role in the campaign for Catholic emancipation and in 1825 he purchased the Waterford Chronicle newspaper to champion this cause. Having been sued for something he published in the Chronicle, he decided to travel Europe rather than pay the damages. Upon his return in 1830, he set about reviving interest in Irish culture. Barron planned to found a college to teach aspects of Irish culture, as well as history, the classics, mathematics and languages. The college would initially be bilingual but he hoped that in time, all subjects would be taught through Irish. His aunt provided a site for the college at Seafield, between Stradbally and Bunmahon. The college opened on New Year's Day 1835 but survived for a mere six months; Barron had a mortgage from a local family which he became unable to pay, the family foreclosed the mortgage and the college was demolished. Philip Barron died an exile in London less than a decade later.

Durrow Hall

In a field beside the level crossing at Durrow is a small shed with a tin roof. This

215. Durrow Station, which served nearby Stradbally, c.1966.

216. The Ballyvoile tunnel is an iconic feature of the Waterford Greenway.

modest building is the old Durrow Hall, once a hub of social activity in the area. In the 1920s the hall was the scene of regular dances, dramatic performances and whist drives. It was also home to the Durrow Amateur Dramatic Club, one of the leading members of which was local schoolteacher Jessie Sim. The following report from the *Dungarvan Observer* of 12 February 1927 is typical:

A very successful Whist Drive followed by a short dance took place at Durrow Hall on last Sunday night. The entire proceedings were admirably conducted by a special committee of the members of the local Handball Club, which included Messrs. Jas. Fleming, Pat Burke, John Drohan, James Curran, John Mansfield, Wm. Cronin and Wm. Power. Light refreshments were provided by Mrs. Fleming. All present were highly pleased with the excellent entertainment experienced.

Durrow Station

The first train pulled into Durrow Station on the morning of 12 August 1878. Now derelict, the station consists of two platforms, a station house and signal cabin. For the ninety or so years of its existence, the station was a link between Stradbally and the world. From here, local produce such as butter and eggs was transported to London. It was also where many emigrants to England and further afield bade farewell to their families. The following story illustrates this link well:

One Christmas Eve in the 1920s, a father rode his pony and trap the few miles journey to Durrow Station to collect his son who had emigrated to England the previous September to look for work. He was only to be disappointed. There had been no

correspondence from the son. The journey to meet the express train in Durrow was more in hope than in expectation. It was not an unusual event around Christmas at that time.

Ballyvoile tunnel

A quarter of a mile in length, the tunnel at Ballyvoile is one of the most striking locations on the Greenway. Completed in 1878, the tunnel was built by miners from Bunmahon, where a large copper-mining operation had recently closed. The tunnel is barrel vaulted with brick and stone, and arched alcoves are set into the walls at intervals – these provided refuge from passing trains. In the 150 years since the tunnel was built, some of the alcoves have developed impressive calcite deposits. The approach to the tunnel at both ends is also noteworthy, as the lush foliage in the cutting is evocative of a tropical rainforest.

The Durrow engagement

During the Irish War of Independence (1919-21), the existing British judicial system was largely replaced by an alternative system of republican courts. For the official system to function at all, it became necessary for courts to get jurors from elsewhere in the country. On the morning of 3 March 1921, a train carrying jurors to the spring assizes in Waterford was held up by the Irish Republican Army (IRA) at Millerstown, about a mile north of Durrow Station. The jurors were ordered off and the train proceeded to Waterford. Meanwhile, the West Waterford IRA active service unit (a mobile armed unit known as a flying column) led by George Lennon lay in wait at the railway line beside the road at Ballyvoile, between the tunnel and the viaduct – they anticipated that the British garrison in Dungarvan would send troops by road to Durrow when word reached them of the train hold-up, thereby creating an ideal ambush situation. Around noon a train approached, carrying troops from Fermoy. The ambush party fired on the train as it passed, but it kept going. Lennon proposed they follow the train to Durrow. Shortly after they had vacated the position, the anticipated troops from Dungarvan passed by on the road. When the column reached Durrow, Lennon divided them into small groups to go in search of food. Some time later, one of these groups spotted a large body of British troops at Durrow Station. The group opened fire, and were soon joined by the rest of the column. A long battle followed. The British retreated to the co-operative store at the rear of the station, and the two groups exchanged intermittent fire. The IRA decided against a direct attack on the co-op as the terrain was exposed and their ammunition was running low, and towards evening they retired north-west to Comeragh. At least one of the column, Andy Kirwan, was wounded by machine-gun fire. Three British soldiers were also wounded.

217. Easter commemoration for Volunteer John Cummins, c.1955.

The Ballylinch ambush

On the morning of 29 April 1921 George Lennon, having heard that a train carrying troops was on its way from Waterford to Dungarvan, mobilised two members of his flying column - Michael Cummins and Mick Morrissey - and proceeded with them to Ballyvoile. They fired on the train as it passed but it did not stop. The ambush party, having grown to nine in number, headed eastwards to the level crossing at Ballylinch. They closed the level crossing gates and affixed a red flag to them to halt the oncoming train, then took up positions on either side of the railway line (the gatekeeper was warned not to open the gates). The British authorities, on their guard after the shooting at Ballyvoile that morning, seemed to be expecting an ambush: the train from Fermoy that evening had a military carriage attached to it with an officer and fifteen to twenty soldiers. Also on the train were several understandably nervous civilians. The train was escorted by an RAF Bristol Fighter aeroplane from Fermoy, which turned back at Ballyvoile tunnel as it was low on fuel. At about 6.40 p.m. the train slowed to a halt at Ballylinch, the ambush party opened fire and for about half an hour a heavy battle ensued. The passengers lay on the floor of the train in terror, and several had very narrow escapes. One IRA volunteer, Paddy Joe Power, was wounded, along with at least one British soldier who had been manning a machine gun, though precise casualty details are unclear. At length the ambush party withdrew - attempts by the soldiers to capture them were in vain - and the train pulled out after a two-hour delay and proceeded to Waterford.

The Ballyvoile ambush

The Ballyvoile ambush took place on 5 June 1921, near the end of the Irish War of Independence. A cycle column of the East Kent Regiment (known as the Buffs) had stayed in Stradbally the night before and were returning to Dungarvan. Members of the Second Battalion, West Waterford Brigade IRA decided to ambush them. The ambush party was led by the battalion's commanding officer, Tom Keating, and Jack Tobin. The initial ambush position was at Kilminin Cross, not far from Stradbally. A woman who lived nearby gave the men a bucket of tea and a bucket of boiled eggs and they had a picnic at the side of the road. The ambush party sent a local girl as a scout to see which route the cycle column were taking back to Dungarvan; she returned

218. Volunteer John Cummins, IRA.

with the news that they were taking the coast road via Ballyvoile. The ambush party rapidly made for Ballyvoile, where they took up position on the railway line at the point where it runs parallel with the road.

The ambush was not a success. It seems the British forces spotted one of the scouts and opened fire on him, at which one of the ambush party opened fire on the British, giving away their position. Many of the ambush party had not seen active service before, and were mostly armed with shotguns, which were ineffective at the range the British were firing from. The IRA were forced to retreat, carrying with them two wounded. The one fatality was 23-year-old Volunteer John (Jack) Cummins of Ballyvoile. Accounts vary, but it seems that Cummins was shot climbing over a wire fence at the side of the railway and fell into the ditch behind the fence. Two members of the cycle column, Lieutenant Oliver and Sergeant Barton, were coming along the ditch in the aftermath of the ambush when they saw him lying in front of them. When they were about fifteen yards away Barton fired, killing Cummins (they claimed he had levelled a shotgun at them). Cummins's body was brought to Dungarvan Barracks and then by train to Fermoy, where a military inquiry was held, before being returned to his family for burial in the Catholic graveyard in Stradbally.

The ambush was later commemorated in song *(The Ballyvoile Ambush)* by Ballyvoile man Jack Daly, grandfather of the singer Kate Bush. Unlike many other such locations around the country, the site of the ambush is very well preserved, with the ditch where Cummins was shot almost perfectly intact. The spot is marked by a white iron cross made by Cummins's IRA comrade Tommy Hallahan; he is also commemorated by a stone plaque on the road below.

Destruction of bridges at Ballyvoile

The main road bridge over the River Dalligan at Ballyvoile (not to be confused with its smaller counterpart downriver at Ballyvoile Cove) was built between 1860 and 1862, under the supervision of a Mr Tarant. Beside it was built a nine-arch railway viaduct which rose 33 metres above the river. The viaduct was completed by 1878.

This viaduct was destroyed during the Irish Civil War (28 June 1922 – 24 May 1923) which followed the Irish War of Independence. The forces of the fledgling Irish Free State founded after the signing of the treaty with Britain fought more hardline Irish republicans who opposed the treaty. Many of those who fought on both sides of the conflict had been members of the IRA during the War of Independence. On the evening of 4 August 1922, members of the anti-Treaty IRA stationed in Dungarvan Castle blew up the centre arch of the road bridge and one of the arches of the viaduct, in an attempt to prevent the National Army from entering Dungarvan. The following days saw the collapse, arch by arch, of almost the entire viaduct (the sole remaining arch was blown up when work began on the new viaduct). It was said that the fish in the river were poisoned by the lime from the masonry from the viaduct. The road bridge was saved by the quick intervention of the County Surveyor, Mr Bowen, who stabilised it with wooden supports, a hazardous job for those involved. It was said that in so doing, Bowen saved the

TRAIN OVER VIADUCT
AT BALLYVOILE,
CO. WATERFORD.
JANY. 31st, 1923.

219. The wreckage of Locomotive No. 189, Ballyvoile viaduct, February 1923.

220. Repairing Ballyvoile road bridge, blown up by the anti-Treaty IRA during the Irish Civil War, July 1923.

ratepayers of the county an outlay of £8,000. The bridge reopened in August 1923. Local newspapers reported that 'The first vehicle to cross over the bridge was a float driven by Mr. Thomas Beatty with a load of goods from Durrow railway station'.

Further sabotage at the viaduct occurred on the evening of 31 January 1923. A breakdown train from Waterford had been removing wreckage caused by a recent derailment near Durrow Station. Shortly before 4.00 p.m., the work completed, the train was about to return to Waterford when it was surrounded by armed members of the IRA. The occupants – District Inspector Mr Purdon, Loco Inspector Mr Capsey, and about twenty repair men – were ordered off. The train was sent backwards through the tunnel towards Durrow to build up steam, then forwards – driverless – to Ballyvoile. The locomotive and the portion of the train nearest it plunged over the precipice, landing upside down in the valley below. The train must have been travelling quite slowly however, as four wagons and the workmen's coach remained hanging over the edge. Unsurprisingly, the locomotive was later scrapped. Thomas Keohan's photographs of the destruction at Ballyvoile were published in newspapers all around the world – he later joked that the one of the train hanging over the edge paid for his wedding!

221. Ballyvoile viaduct with Helvick Head in the background.

222. The train hangs over Ballyvoile viaduct, February 1923.

The replacement viaduct at Ballyvoile was built by the McAlpine construction firm (made famous by the ballad *McAlpine's Fusiliers*) with local labour, and it is said that many of these men later worked for McAlpine in England. Work commenced in October 1923. Although the Civil War was over, the work was guarded by soldiers, who slept in railway carriages on site. The new viaduct, consisting of metal girders supported by three concrete piers, opened in June 1924. While it has since become a landmark in its own right, it lacks the grace and elegance of its predecessor.

The Copper Coast UNESCO Global Geopark

The Copper Coast is a beautiful, rugged corner of south-east Ireland, stretching for about 20 km from Stradbally eastwards towards Tramore. There are at least nine easily accessible, individual and charming beaches, coves or harbours along the Copper Coast. They are all different shapes and sizes – some with excellent surfing conditions, some perfect lazing locations, some have glorious rock pools rich in colourful seaweeds, fish, shrimps, sea anemones and a world to be explored and most are overlooked by spectacular cliffs of

223. The Copper Coast is a UNESCO Global Geopark.

varying colours and structures. Each beach is slightly different every day, indeed every hour, as the tides come and go, the wind wafts or roars, the sea tinkles or thunders.

The beaches include: Stradbally, a deep horseshoe-shaped cove where the sand seems to go out forever at low tide; Ballydwan – great high cliffs of different colours and a sea-stack with a story; Boatstrand harbour – fishing, swimming, boating, and fun for families; Annestown – sand, pools, surf, more families, more fun; and Kilfarrasy – sand, rocks, and a great place to explore from by kayak.
Also within the area are seven villages, each with its own character and heritage: Stradbally, picture-perfect with its medieval church ruins, great house and estate, a couple of pubs, shop and thatched cottages; Bunmahon with its mining and social history and a visitor centre to tell the tale; Kill with two pubs, a restaurant and a shop; Boatstrand with its harbour; Fenor with its pub, mini-farm, and a fascinating short nature walk over a fen (and look out for the angels!); and Dunhill with a shop, pub, ruined castle and church, and magical valley walk. And the more you explore the more you find – boreens, lakes, dolmens, standing stones and more long-forgotten churches with gravestones to be peered at and wondered about.

The Copper Coast is a UNESCO Global Geopark, a designation earned by its obvious and open geology, as seen in the spectacular and varied cliffs and rocks which face the sea, its mining heritage, and the ongoing work to join all of this up. By raising awareness of the importance of the area's geological heritage in history and society today, UNESCO Global Geoparks aim to give local people a sense of pride in their region and strengthen their identification with the area. They also try to develop tourism sustainably, highlighting the human and earth (geo/gaia) heritage of the territory.

The Copper Coast Geopark Visitor Centre

The centre occupies the former Monksland Church of Ireland church on the outskirts of Bunmahon village. The church was built during the period of intense copper mining in the area but closed due to dwindling parishioner numbers in 1937. The Geopark acquired the building, which was in quite poor condition, in 2008 and with the help of Leader funding restored it to use as a visitor centre with a café and for community events and meetings.

In the café you can eat decadent cakes and rustic sandwiches bursting with real tastes and drink excellent coffee. In the little shop you may find a locally made memento of your visit to the area.

The exhibition tells various stories about the area, principally related to the mining period, social as well as industrial, but also of others who lived on or passed through the Copper Coast. Of course there is also geology-made-fascinating including a seismometer and a sandbox.

Further reading

Tom Hickey, John Keane and Brian Corry, *Stradbally na Déise II* (2013)

Fachtna Ó Drisceoil, *The Missing Postman: What really happened to Larry Griffin?* (2011)

Tom Cunningham, Robin Aherne and Tomás P. Ó Floinn (eds), *Stradbally G.A.A. / C.L.G. Sráidbhaile na nDéise, 1886-2016: An illustrated history* (2016)

224. Ballyvoile Cove c.1950.

225. Ballyvoile Cove

KILMACTHOMAS

A mill town in the heart of Co. Waterford.

302. Main Street, Kilmacthomas c.1900.

During the Middle Ages, the River Mahon formed the boundary between the territory of the Powers of Curraghmore (to the north and east) and that of the FitzGeralds, Earls of Desmond (to the west and south). At this important river crossing, which was often disputed between the two families, a castle was built.

The old name for the townland was Kilcool (Cill Choill, the church by the wood). The name Kilmacthomas (Coill Mhic Thomáis Fhinn, the wood of the son of fair-haired Thomas) is derived from a member of the Power family who lived there. A deed in the archives at Curraghmore dated 12 July 1472 records that Thomas son of Thomasyn Poer of Kylcoill had granted to Richard, son of Nicholas Poer (head of the Curraghmore family) and his heirs 'Kylcoill alias Kylmcthomasyn' and other lands.

In 1529 the Earl of Desmond and FitzGerald of Dromana signed a peace treaty. One of its terms was that they would join forces 'to attack and recover the Castle of Kyllmacthomasyn' – but they never did.

After the rebellion of the Earl of Desmond and his followers was crushed in the 1580s, their vast estates were confiscated. Kilmacthomas was granted to Sir Christopher Hatton, Lord Chancellor of England, who died

303. Main Street, Kilmacthomas c.1900.

soon afterwards. Kilmacthomas was then granted to the Knowles family, but the Powers still claimed to be the rightful owners: in 1600 Henry Knowles complained to the government that Lord Power had 'entered upon my castle, seized my goods to the value of £300, and turned my wife and six small children out of doors without anything earthly to relieve them'.

In 1605 Lord Power was granted a licence to hold a market every Thursday and two annual fairs at Kilmacthomas, 'to the intent that the inhabitants ... be the easier brought to a civil and human sort of life'.

During the wars of the 1640s, the castle changed hands several times. In 1643 it was besieged by an English force under Sir Charles Vavasour. When the Irish garrison fired on the besiegers, some of the English soldiers broke ranks, burned the thatched houses beside the castle, and attacked under cover of the smoke. The civilians who had taken refuge in the castle ran out in a panic 'and were by our soldiers knocked on the head'. The garrison then surrendered upon being given quarter and were allowed to leave. On the night of 2 December 1649, the army of Oliver Cromwell reached Kilmacthomas. He had failed to capture Waterford and his soldiers were cold, sick, exhausted and demoralised by

304. Main Street, Kilmacthomas c.1900.

305. *The view from Kilmacthomas Station towards the Comeragh Mountains c.1975.*

the continuing heavy rain. It took them a whole day to reach Kilmacthomas, 'it being' (as Cromwell wrote) 'as terrible a day as ever I marched in, in all my life'. They had hoped to find safety and supplies there, but 'we had to many scarce straw, food, or firing, being deceived in reports of the place'. It took them the whole of the next day to ford the swollen River Mahon, and they then marched drearily on towards Dungarvan.

The Civil Survey of 1654 reported of Kilmacthomas that 'there is a Castle and a bawne [fortified enclosure] uppon the land'. The castle was still in existence in the 18th century but was demolished soon after. In 1841 John O'Donovan reported for the Ordnance Survey: 'This castle is now totally destroyed and the

bank on which it stood about 30 yards to the north-east of the bridge on the east side of the river is nearly cut away for the purpose of obtaining gravel for the roads'.

Sir Richard Cox (1650-1733), Chief Justice of the Common Pleas 1701-3 and Lord Chancellor of Ireland 1703-4, described Kilmacthomas around 1685 as:

An old village and a strong castle (where last yeare was built a County house for a quarter sessions) on the banks of the river, formerly the seat of Mc Thomas, a great man in this country. Not far from it are the mountains of Comrah, soe called from the village Comrah on the east side thereof.

306. Kilmacthomas c.1910. The woollen mill is to the left of the image.

The Civil Survey of 1654 notes that the village was on the site of lands owned by 'James Walsh of Ilandbegg, Irish Papist deceased … whereon standeth the wales of several ruined howses and a paved streete intended before the rebellion for a Plantacon'. In 1746 the historian Charles Smith referred to this settlement which he said was 'planned by one Greatrakes'. Smith mentions the 'ancient castle' and the barrack which housed twenty men. In 1790 the Marquess of Waterford built the great causeway linking Kilmacthomas with Graigueshoneen. He also built a new forge on the 'Old Road' which has a distinctive cut-stone façade with a doorway in the shape of a horseshoe.

In 1824 the Revd Richard Ryland in his history of Waterford city and county referred to the 'handsome stone bridge' in Kilmacthomas which crossed the River Mahon and made the village more accessible.

As Kilmacthomas was a stopping-point for those travelling from Waterford city through to the west of the county, it attracted comment from many travel writers.

In the autumn of 1835 the English travel writer John Barrow went on a tour around Ireland. He encountered an interesting sight at Kilmacthomas:

We met a great concourse of people, who seemed to have assembled to witness a sort of cross-country race, something resembling a steeplechase; and on proceeding a few yards further, I observed in the distance

307. Kilmacthomas Post Office c.1900.

308. The seven-arch Kilmacthomas viaduct was opened in 1878.

another large assemblage ... The latter turned out to be a funeral procession of some wealthy farmer. It was the most numerously attended, and, from the number of horsemen ... the most respectable of any I have seen in Ireland ... The coffin was under a canopy displayed to view, and, huddled up at each end of it sat two old women, whom I suppose to have been keeners. They had the best of it, as it happened to be raining, as usual.

Samuel Lewis described the village in 1837 in his Topographical Dictionary of Ireland. With a population of 982 people, it had a dispensary and was the county headquarters of the constabulary police.

In 1842 the novelist William Makepeace Thackeray came through the village noting that one could change horses there and that the road was crowded with carts full of seaweed brought from the coast to be used as fertiliser. The historian Thomas Carlyle, passed through Kilmacthomas in July 1849 and described it as a 'clear white village

309. Shanahan family belongings thrown into the yard during their eviction, 17 November 1887.

hanging on the steep declivity ... a poor small place with houses or huts all limewashed, street torn up by rain streams. Lives very bright with me yet, as seen in the bright summer afternoon'.

Archibald Stark arrived in Kilmacthomas in 1850 and was very taken by a young lady he met in the post office:

I penetrated to the kitchen of the post office and lit a cigar. A huge pot hung over the fire, which was fed with bramble bushes and mountain heather ... by a comely damsel, who might have sat for one of Sir Walter Scott's heroines. This rustic beauty, with modest sweetness which no professor of deportment could impart, invited the traveller to take a seat and warm himself... Strange, is it not, that Irish women, in the rural districts, retain their good looks and pure complexion, notwithstanding the privations they frequently endure, and that they spend so much of their time in an atmosphere of turf smoke?

The Kilmacthomas fair was reported in the Waterford Standard in May 1870 as follows:

310. Constabulary in attendance at the Shanahan eviction, 17 November 1887.

The most striking feature of this fair is the immense number of farm servants that present themselves on the grass for 12 months engagement. The wages of the men servants for the twelve months ranged from 5 to 18 pounds with diet and lodging. Female servants from 5.10s to 6.10s. The priests denounced this system. There were as usual a goodly supply of gamblers on the green. The votaries of Bacchus might be counted by hundreds, at the supply of drinks as follows: 150 barrels of beer, 200 gallons of whiskey, and 3,000 bottles of porter.

The coming of the railway in 1877, bringing direct access to the outside world, ended Kilmacthomas's days as a sleepy backwater. It encouraged local entrepreneurs to set up in business: Dunn's (Flahavan's), Hill's, Kiersey's, Canny's (Kirwan's) and Reilly's were enabled to sell agricultural goods directly to anywhere in Britain and Ireland.

A very well-documented eviction took place at Shanahan's of Scrahan, Kilmacthomas on 17 November 1887. On the morning of the proposed eviction, about 200 policemen assembled in Kilmacthomas under the command of County Inspector James Whelan and magistrates Captain Owen Slacke and Mr Dunsterville. Most had arrived by train from Waterford. Their job for the day was to protect sub-sheriff John T. Hudson, chief bailiff Johnny 'Shauneen' Kirwan, and seven or eight other bailiffs. The party marched to Scrahan with the Curraghmore battering ram. They were met by a large hostile crowd led by Fr Comerford PP, Fr Condon CC, Fr Power of Mothel, the solicitor L.F. Strange, Chairman of the Kilmacthomas Board of Guardians James Power, David Gleeson PLG, David Kiersey PLG, L. Power PLG, and William Fisher PC. Members of the press were also present; Richard

311. Main Street, Kilmacthomas c.1935.

Edward Brenan of Dungarvan was there to photograph the unhappy scene. There were several violent altercations between members of the crowd and the eviction party, but the eviction was completed by about 1.00 p.m. The house remained untenanted and the Shanahans were able to return in 1904 when the Marquess of Waterford sold the property along with other land in the area.

A number of notable people are associated with Kilmacthomas.

The Gaelic poet Donncha Rua Mac Conmara lived in the village and is buried in Newtown Graveyard. Another Gaelic scholar was Seán Ó Ciarghusa (Kiersey), who was born at Kilnagrange Mills (now Flahavan's).

If we take a quick tour of the village we can start at the square where the hotel (now a supermarket) once stood. Daniel O'Connell, the Liberator, addressed the crowds from one of its windows during the 1826 general election (in which Catholic emancipation was the pressing issue). On Sunday 18 June 1826 Daniel O'Connell, Henry Villiers Stuart and Fr Roger Murphy began a grand tour of the county in Kilmacthomas. O'Connell described it for his wife:

We heard an early Mass at Waterford and then started for Dungarvan. We breakfasted at Kilmacthomas, a town belonging to the Beresfords, but the people belong to us. They came out to meet us with green boughs and such shouting you can have no idea of. I harangued them from the window of the inn, and we had a good deal of laughing at the

312. Kilmacthomas Station, 1 June 1975.

bloody Beresfords. Judge what the popular feeling must be when in this, a Beresford town, every man their tenant, we had such a reception.

Continuing down under the railway bridge, we pass the house on Main Street (now Halloran's shop) which was the reputed birthplace in 1797 of the actor William Grattan Tyrone Power. His great-grandson was the film star Tyrone Power. He came to Dublin to film *The Rising of the Moon* in 1957 and took a week's break from filming to visit the village of his ancestors. He was disappointed as he walked up and down the street and very few people recognised him. The local postman Michael Murphy got his autograph on the back of a photograph. Power returned to finish the film, which was made at Ardmore Studios. In the subsequent promotion of the film, he announced that he was from a small village in southern Ireland called Kilmacthomas.

Coming up Main Street we come to Kiersey's (Keighery's). This was originally Donoghue's, who were agents for the White Star Line. It was here that Frank Dwan of Bunmahon bought the ticket for his ill-fated voyage on the *Titanic*; he was the oldest Irish passenger to perish.

Thomas Maher of Main Street was a great horseman in the 1950s. He took part in many films made in England such as *The Black Arrow* (1948), *Ivanhoe* (1952) and *Knights of the Round Table* (1953).

The Kirwan brothers, Percy and Rody, were natives of Kilmacthomas and achieved great fame in athletics all over the world. Percy (1881-1969) was a judge at the Olympic Games and British champion long jumper in 1910, 1911 and 1912. He attended every Olympic Games from 1924 to 1960. In 2001 the bypass bridge over the River Mahon was named after him; in 2012 a plaque was erected to his memory on the family business on Main Street. Rody is credited with bringing toe-to-hand football to Kerry (with whom he won an All-Ireland medal in the early part of the last century).

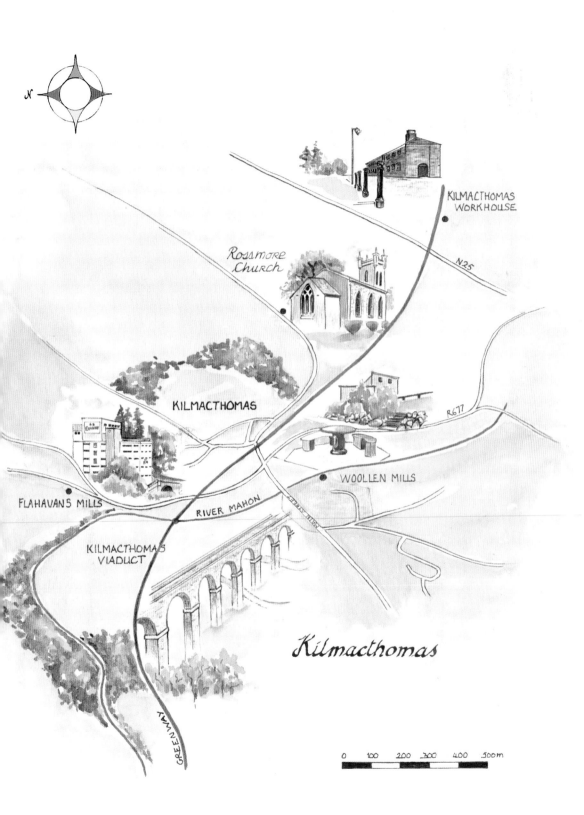

N

KILMACTHOMAS
WORKHOUSE

N25

Rossmore
Church

R677

KILMACTHOMAS

WOOLLEN MILLS

FLAHAVANS MILLS

RIVER MAHON

KILMACTHOMAS
VIADUCT

GREENWAY

Kilmacthomas

0   100   200 300   400   500m

313. Map of Kilmacthomas.

Kilmacthomas Woollen Mill

The development of a woollen mill in the mid-19th century by the Marquess and Marchioness of Waterford provided an economic boost in the area. The River Mahon was an ideal source of power to turn the mill wheels. In addition to opening a factory, the marchioness planted trees along the village streets and these are visible in postcard views from the early 20th century.

In 1850 Louisa, Lady Waterford, wife of Henry Beresford, 3rd Marquis of Waterford, set up a weaving and clothes-manufacturing business in a house in Kilmacthomas to give employment to the local girls. She acquired a number of old spinning jennies and looms to make white flannel. A clothes club was set up: anyone who contributed one penny per week could purchase cloth at double the value of their money. This was a significant initiative, as can be seen from the fact that many travel writers noted the rags the people wore. She imported cotton from Lancashire and encouraged her friends to buy the finished products. As the industry developed, the girls started to weave in colours. The mill later mainly produced woollen goods and thirty women were employed under the direction of one Anthony Thomas. Blankets produced by the mill won a medal at the Great Exhibition in Dublin in 1853. In March 1859, Louisa and her husband visited the mill and promised to upgrade the equipment; however, he was killed in a hunting accident the next

314. Workers at the Marquess of Waterford's woollen mill, Kilmacthomas c.1905.

day. Louisa had to vacate Curraghmore and went to live in England, but the factory remained in production. The mill building was extended in 1879.

In 1884 it was noted that a third of the factory was idle and that there was about £20,000 invested in buildings, machinery and stock. The women were paid from six to eight shillings per week and were employed throughout the year. Mr Abbott was the manager and the Revd John F. Parker, Rector of Kilmacthomas, was the honorary treasurer. *The Irish Times* noted that '[t]he wool is chiefly bought through a Dublin firm ... It is first sorted, then cleaned by an ingenious process, dyed, carded, and turned out as untwisted thread. From the carding machine it is sent to the mule, where it is drawn out to the requisite thinness and then twisted.' The water-powered mill was supplemented with a horizontal 20-horsepower engine acquired from a firm in Glasgow.

The Irish Times published an advertisement in 1896 for Kilmacthomas tweeds which were described as 'unsurpassed for durability, purity and design'. The following year, it was noted that the fabrics 'are fast becoming the rage with connoisseurs in tweed suits. Wherever an outfit in hunting, shooting and cycling etc., is required, the material of these mills is sure to be selected'. The mill had a range of twenty-two items at this time.

315. *The weaving department of the woollen mill, Kilmacthomas c.1905.*

316. Kilmacthomas Workhouse, built in 1851.

In January 1909 the *Cork Examiner* reported that Lord Waterford's employees at the woollen mill were entertained to a sumptuous New Year's Eve supper, concert and ball. 'The entertainment was held in the warehouse … which was cleared out and beautifully decorated for the occasion. A platform was erected, and the workers sat down to supper at three long tables'. After supper James Carruthers junior, the son of the manager, played the titular role in a sketch entitled *The Colonel's Consent*. This was followed by a dance which continued until 5.00 a.m.

In 1910 it was reported that Lord Waterford was upgrading the machinery and buildings. The weavers were paid one shilling a day and worked from 6.30 a.m. to 6.00 p.m.

In 1920 Lord Waterford sold the factory to a Mr Stephenson who did not retain the operation for long. It was acquired by Flahavan's and operated as a grain store and drying facility. In June 1930 the *Waterford Standard* reported that the mill had been closed for ten years and was about to be acquired by a 'well known Cork firm'.

Many local families originally came to Kilmacthomas to work in the mill such as the Stack, Thompson and Collins families.

Flahavan's Mill

In 1785 Thomas Dunn, great-great-great-grandfather of the present owner, was running a mill on this site. In 1902, Edward Flahavan built the present family home adjacent to the mill. The mill was expanded in 1935 and an oat-flaking facility installed. By 1959 the current building was complete.

Kilmacthomas Workhouse

As it did all across the county, the Famine had a dramatic impact on the people of Kilmacthomas. In 1846 the *Cork Examiner* reported on the destruction of forty-six homes at Graigueshoneen, Kilmacthomas owned by the Marquess of Waterford. Each family was offered £2 to vacate their home, which they did, and this amounted to 227 people in total. On 19 September a meeting was advertised in the local press to take place in Kilmacthomas, the purpose of which was to organise a Female Tenant League. The letter noted that women had seen their families reduced to 'walking skeletons, by oppression and wrong; they are now little better than moving spectres and a living mass of bare bones, slowly sinking into the welcome grave'. The League was intended to galvanise the women of Ireland to join together in a united movement: 'We'll shame the men into action'. In 1848 the Waterford city Board of Guardians opened a temporary fever hospital there.

The Kilmacthomas workhouse was built in 1851 (after those at Lismore and Dungarvan) in the townland of Carrignanonshagh (Carraig na nÓinseach, rock of the female idiots), on the Waterford side of Kilmacthomas. Before this, local people had to go to the workhouse at Waterford or Dungarvan. Its architect was George Wilkinson, who designed a building with a pleasant outward appearance, with mullioned windows and gabled roofs. Inside, however, bleakness and austerity was what the Poor Law Commissioners desired, to discourage all but the utterly destitute from entry. To further repel those seeking aid, the workhouse regime was one of order, constant occupation, constant and harsh regulation, and the 'exclusion of all vulgar habits and tempting excitements'. The purpose of the workhouses was to replace outdoor relief for paupers. In order to receive a minimum level of food and shelter, the destitute had to abandon their cabins and potato patches, surrendering their possessions. Once inside the workhouse, to further add to their humiliation and discomfort, families were broken up: boys to the boys' quarters, men with the men, girls with the girls and so on; only infants were allowed to stay with nursing mothers.

The site for the workhouse was purchased from Mr Power O'Shee of Gardenmorris and the house was built to accommodate 600 inmates at a cost of £14,818. The infirmary was built as part of the workhouse and catered for the sick of the area. Conditions in the infirmary were very primitive at the opening of the workhouse. In 1853 the medical officer, Dr John Coghlan, reported that '[b]edsteads are urgently required for the infirmary, as the straw stuffed ticks that lie on the floor [are] required to be lifted off the ground, both for circulation of air and to allow the floor to be washed'. Fifty trestle beds were ordered for the infirmary at a cost of ten shillings each. These bedsteads had no headboards, and patients rested against the bare damp walls of the ward.

Patients suffering from fever – typhus or cholera – had to be removed to Waterford in a special horse-drawn van until the fever shed was erected at the back of the workhouse. In 1853, Dr Coghlan recommended that the van for removing fever patients to Waterford be fitted with sliding panels to allow circulation of fresh air and also be painted a light colour to make it less gloomy and to render it cooler in summer.

When the workhouse opened, the school was supported by private subscriptions. In 1853, the Revd John F. Parker applied for the poor rate for the support of the school and teachers and this was granted in due course.

Religious instruction formed a large part of the curriculum in the beginning, with both the Catholic and Protestant clergy ensuring that they were given their fair share of the school time. Differences in religion were respected, but any child who was abandoned or deserted by their parents at the workhouse had to be registered as a Protestant, so there were several differences of opinion between the master and Catholic parish priest. Usually the parish priest tried to have an abandoned child taken out and cared for in a Catholic household.

The plan of the workhouse did not have a chapel incorporated into it, but in 1853 the Revd R. Power, Catholic chaplain, requested the Board of Guardians to erect an altar and supply requisites for saying Mass. A section of the dining hall was screened off for this purpose.

Any inmate who died in the workhouse was interred in the workhouse graveyard, which adjoined the workhouse land, unless relatives or friends claimed the body for burial in the deceased's own parish graveyard.

Coffins were ordered by the dozen. A requisition order for coffins would read thus: '4 Coffins size 1 @ 3/6 each, 4 Coffins size 2 @ 5/- each, 4 Coffins size 3 @ 6/6 each'.

An interesting extract from the minute books of the Kilmacthomas Poor Law Union reads as follows: 'John Burke who died in the house lately left a small trunk and two pretty good coats. One of the coats would be suitable and useful for the gatekeeper and the other would be serviceable for the man going out with the ambulance.'

Another extract from March 1859 also gives an idea of the living conditions of inmates: 'An inmate of the house has got employment on condition that the Guardians would give him a suit of clothes. The boy when admitted had only petticoats on. Allowed not to exceed 12/-.'

The Sisters of St John of God came from the mother house in New Ross to take over nursing care in the workhouse fever hospital in May 1873. This made Kilmacthomas the second workhouse in Ireland to have nuns as nurses. These were the first nuns to come to Kilmacthomas. The Mercy sisters came from Cappoquin and taught and nursed in the workhouse when the St John of God sisters left the hospital.

The workhouse closed in September 1919. At this time, most of the inmates were aged and infirm and so the Board of Guardians thought it would be more economical to close Kilmacthomas workhouse and to have the inmates transferred to Dungarvan or Lismore (see Una Troy's 1960 novel The Workhouse Graces). They considered the workhouse to be a great burden on the rates, and that if it was closed they, the ratepayers, would never again see a poor day.

The workhouse remained idle for a few years after this and was then taken over

317. The bridge over the N25 outside Kilmacthomas.

as a barracks by the anti-Treaty IRA in 1922. They were about to blow it up, but the nuns beseeched them not to do so, and shortly afterwards the Free State Army took it as their barracks. For years afterwards, certain small apartments of the house were let to tenants awaiting cottages from the Board of Health.

The Convent of Mercy

The Convent of Mercy of the Holy Cross, Kilmacthomas, was founded in 1881. It owes its establishment to the unfailing zeal of Fr David Hearne, then curate of the parish. The architect for the new convent, church and school was Mathias T. O'Keefe of Cork. His design included a beautiful Gothic church measuring 75 feet by 24 feet. It was to be built of local stone with a limestone dressing. The belfry was to have been topped with a narrow spire 80 feet high capped with a weathervane.

All this was to cost £3,000; the funds were raised by private subscription. The Marquess of Waterford donated the site for the project and the work was given to the contractor Edward Shimmick of Cork. The school was to house senior, junior and infant sections. A music room, a fine entrance hall and cloakroom were planned; a pay school or private school was also included. It appears that Shimmick became bankrupt during the construction and could not complete the contract; the sisters employed Thomas Flynn of Waterford to finish the job.

The building of the convent was completed according to plan, but it then became apparent that the funds had run out. The community thus found themselves with a convent and no church. Fr Hearne came up with the idea of building a temporary church. He got the materials from the buildings of the then-defunct Bunmahon mines, using

318. The Convent of Mercy with temporary church to the right of the photo c.1910.

these to erect a chapel on the site of the proposed stone church. This temporary chapel lasted until quite recently, serving both the convent and the people of Kilmacthomas.

Rossmire Church of Ireland church

The Church of Ireland church stands just beyond Rossmire House, on the outskirts of the village. Built in 1829 on the site of an earlier church, its design is simple, with a west tower and small sanctuary. The interior was remodelled c.1880. The church is also known as St John's but it is unclear if this is an official dedication. The association with St John is an old one: in the field to the south of the church is an ancient well known as St John's Well. The graveyard contains memorials dating from the 18th century.

The Fair Green

This large open space was used for the annual hiring fair held annually on 12 May. Those wishing to be hired would stand at the fair and be inspected by prospective bosses. Michael Terry from Ring was hired at this fair and he described the scene in his book Beatha Mhichíl Turraoin (1956):

I got a spin to the train at Durrow. Five pence it cost to go to Kilmacthomas. The first thing I saw at Kilmacthomas was a cish of Carrick Brogues [boots] and I bought a pair. Nine shillings they cost and people went miles just to buy these boots. There was a big gathering at the fair and each tradesman had his own distinctive mark. If you were a dairyman you had a spancel in your hand and if you were a horseman you had a winkers in your hand.

319. Rossmire Church of Ireland church, c.1910.

The farmers could question and bargain hard with you. If you were an all-round man you could get £18 a year.

A butter market was held every Thursday at Kilmacthomas, Tuesday was fowl market day. The butter came in firkins made from sally sticks, each holding 56 lbs. Kiersey's were a major buyer of butter and other buyers were at Morrissey's end of the square. Michael Kiersey of the Mills organised a monthly fair for farm livestock. He was presented with a gold watch and chain by local farmers in appreciation of his work in setting up the fair.

320. Mobile tea van at the Fair Green, Kilmacthomas on fair day c.1910.

321. Employees of Edward Hill's bakery, Kilmacthomas c.1935.

PORTLAW

A 19th-century industrial model village built around a cotton mill.

402. Mayfield Mills, Portlaw, 1884.

Situated just 5 km from the Kilmeaden stage of the Greenway and 15 km from Kilmacthomas is the village of Portlaw. The village lies between Kilmeaden to the east and the River Suir to the north. The hills around Portlaw provide spectacular views of the Suir valley and the breathtaking Comeragh Mountains to the west as you look out over the demesne of Curraghmore, seat of the Marquess of Waterford. The village of Portlaw holds a unique place in the landscape of planned industrial villages as it influenced other industrial developments such as Bessbrook, Co. Armagh and Saltaire in West Yorkshire. For almost 200 years, the factory complex constructed by David Malcomson in the early 19th century provided a backdrop to village life. Built as a cotton mill to manufacture yarn and cloth, in the 20th century it became a tannery, producing leather products fordomestic and export markets. The area's rich heritage includes early monastic settlements in Kilbunny, late medieval fortifications like Rockett's Castle, the large demesne at Curraghmore and a unique industrial past. For more than a century prior to the arrival of the Malcomsons, the two significant families in the locality were the Beresfords of Curraghmore and Mays of Rockett's Castle.

A number of theories for the derivation of the name Portlaw have been suggested. The most credible of these, supported by a number of prominent Gaelic scholars, is that the name is derived from the Irish for 'stony river bank'. While the modern Irish spelling is Portlách, the older version of the spelling, Portcládhach, gives a clue to the word's origin. *Port* is a river bank. The second part of the name *cládhach* has generated the most discussion but it is generally agreed to derive from *cladach* meaning a stony place by a river or the sea. The view from the bridge over the canal and River Clodiagh supports this theory: the river bed is completely covered with small stones.

Archaeological evidence in the area shows that the River Suir and its hinterland

403. Portlaw Bridge, built c.1780. In the background is the Presbyterian church, built in 1820.

was utilised to sustain early settlers. Rivers were also an important method of transport and communication. In the 1970s a *fulacht fia* was found in Darrigle, Portlaw. Mainly constructed between 2,500 and 3,500 years ago, these were used as cooking places by our ancestors. A pit was dug out close to a water source and lined with timber, prior to being filled with water. Stones heated on a fire were placed in the water to bring it to cooking temperature. Meat was then placed in the pit to cook. There are also three standing stones in Kilmovee but their origins are unclear.

One of the earliest communities in the area was centred around the church of St Munna in Kilbunny, built in the 8th century. A noted feature of the church is its 11th-century Irish-Romanesque doorway. (The Irish-Romanesque building style is characterised by flamboyant doorways and elaborate carvings, replacing an earlier, much plainer indigenous Irish church-building form.) At one point it is estimated that there were over 230 monks in the community and that the settlement covered a far larger area than the present church grounds. Located either side of the entrance to the church are two fine examples of bullaun stones. In their time they were used as holy water fonts but their original purpose may have been as mortars for grinding grain. Many people still associate bullaun stones with having healing properties.

The name Poer (later Power) is derived from *le Pohier*, meaning a native of Picardy in north-eastern France. The Waterford Powers descend from a certain Henry le Poer, to whom King John granted in about 1200 a very large estate in east Waterford, which became the feudal barony of Donoyle (*Dún Aill*, the cliff fort) or Dunhill. He appears to have been the son of a Philip le Poer, who held lands near Haverfordwest in Pembrokeshire. The Powers of Dunhill dominated east Waterford during the 13th century and were frequently at war with the citizens of Waterford. By the year 1400 the senior line had died out, and junior branches jostled to fill the vacuum. The leadership passed eventually to the Powers of Curraghmore, who ruled the area like a medieval feoffdom, holding onto the office of sheriff despite the attempts of their enemies to break their rule.

At Curraghmore in the 15th century the Powers erected a strong tower house, which forms the oldest part of the present mansion: the entrance hall and the rooms above it. The older of the two stone bridges over the river Clodiagh, mentioned in the Civil Survey of 1654 as being "not very farr from the said Castle", may also date from this period, but it has been so much altered in later times that it cannot be dated with certainty. On older maps it is marked as "Bullen's Bridge", after William Bullen the head gardener who lived nearby. In the late 19th century it was given the fanciful name of "King John's Bridge".

An interesting artefact from the 16th century is the Portlaw Bell. This small bronze handbell is decorated with columnar figures interspersed with swags, surmounting birds and monkeys. It is inscribed 'ME FECIT IOHANNIES A FINE Ao 1549' ('Johannies à Fine made me in 1549') in Roman capitals around the base. Johannies à Fine was the bronze founder at Malines in Belgium who cast the bell. Commissioned for the family chapel at Curraghmore, it was donated to the old Catholic church in Portlaw. In 1939 it was lent by Dr

404. *Curraghmore House c.1900.*

405. *The Square, Portlaw c.1900.*

Jeremiah Kinane, Catholic Bishop of Waterford and Lismore, to the museum of St Patrick's College, Maynooth; it is now on loan to Waterford Museum of Treasures.

According to legend, Curraghmore survived being confiscated by Oliver Cromwell in 1649 due to the actions of Lady Catherine, daughter of John, 5th Lord Power. The story goes that Lady Catherine lured her father (a known Royalist) into the cellar and locked him there, before going out to meet Cromwell who she invited into the house, plying him with refreshments. Cromwell was so impressed by her hospitality that he agreed to spare Curraghmore, on the condition that she should marry one of his officers. Lady Catherine agreed, the officers were lined up with their backs to her and she had the misfortune to pick a particularly villainous-looking one named Beresford.

In fact, Cromwell never visited Curraghmore, and the Power-Beresford marriage took place almost seventy years later. The real reason that Curraghmore was not confiscated was that Lord Power had been insane for many years and therefore (the Cromwellians reasoned) could not have taken part in the 1641 Rebellion.

The 1654 Civil Survey undertaken by Cromwell's men refers to 'a fayre Castle and a goodly stone house upon the land, there is also an Orchard and Meadow upon the same and stands by the side of a fine wood'. It also mentions 'the River Clodagh running within a musket shot'. The successor to the 5th Lord Power was created Earl of Tyrone in 1673 and Curraghmore remained the seat of the Earls of Tyrone until 1704 when

the 3rd Earl, James, died with no male successor. The estate had done well to survive the vicissitudes of the 17th century. It even survived the 6th Lord Power commanding a regiment in the army of James II, the losing side in the Williamite War (1688–91).

The 3rd Earl's daughter and only child, Lady Catherine, married Sir Marcus Beresford in 1717 and the present family are direct descendants of this union. The marriage joined two influential Irish families. During their tenure there were extensive improvements made to the main house at Curraghmore. Lady Catherine's legacy is the magnificent Shell House in the garden, which she completed in 1754, the date given on her statue there by John van Nost. The huge courtyard was also completed at this time to the design of Waterford's John Roberts. During the reign of Marcus and Catherine's son George, 2nd Earl of Tyrone and 1st Marquess of Waterford, the house was enriched with a splendid suite of rooms designed by James Wyatt in the 1770s.

Another significant local landmark is Rockett's Castle. This tower house, originally called Rokelle's Court, dates from the 15th or 16th century and is unusual in that it is circular (like nearby Ballyclohy Castle). It belonged to the family of de la Rokelle [sic], who had held lands of Gortardagh in the area from the 13th century onwards. In the early 17th century the Rokelles [sic] were heavily in debt and mortgaged their estate to two Waterford merchants named Woodlock and Strang(e). They foreclosed and divided the estate between them, one part being called Gortardagh Woodlock and the other Gortardagh Strange. Both lost their lands under the Commonwealth. Sir Algernon May was granted the Strange estate and his grant was confirmed under the Acts of Settlement and Explanation in 1666. His descendants – who became politically influential in Waterford and nationally in the late 17th and 18th centuries – built a house onto the castle and renamed it Mayfield (see below). In 1795 they sold out to the Revd John Thomas Medlycott. The old house burned down accidentally in the mid-19th century and the present house was then built nearby. The name Rockett's Castle is relatively modern.

Legend has it that one of the original family was a river pirate who, along with some accomplices, captured an English ship and proceeded to raid other ships, dividing the spoils among the locals. Eventually the pirate and his crew were captured, hung, drawn and quartered. It is said that he gave his name to Rockett's Tree, a gallows tree once located on the upper part of the Yellow Road in Waterford city. However, the legend does not seem to have any historical basis whatever.

There are three distinct aspects to the heritage of the modern village of Portlaw: industrial, social and built heritage. The village's structure and layout is based on its relationship with the cotton mill and the Malcomson family.

The Malcomson name became familiar throughout 19th-century Ireland as they grew to be one of the best-known industrial families in the country, influential in milling and shipbuilding. As businesspeople they were deeply influenced by their Quaker ideals. Honest endeavour, religious tolerance, respect and consideration were hallmarks of their interactions with both employees and neighbours. Portlaw village owes its existence to the arrival in the early 1820s of David Malcomson. He leased the site of a flour mill, which had burnt down in 1818, from John Medlycott of Rockett's Castle. It was during his time as manager of the Anner flour mill in Clonmel, and later as owner of the Corporation Mills, that Malcomson generated his wealth. A large part of his fortune was a direct result of the Napoleonic Wars when England needed corn and flour to feed its armies.

With his background in flour milling, it initially seems strange that Malcomson would build a cotton mill. Several factors influenced his decision. He feared that the protectionist Corn Laws, which imposed high tariffs on corn imported from outside the United Kingdom, were going to be repealed, meaning that England could cheaply import corn from further afield. In addition, the end of the Napoleonic Wars had seen the price of flour dramatically decrease. Furthermore, Malcomson was already familiar with Portlaw as he had leased a corn mill and stores at Pouldrew, located between Kilmeaden and Portlaw. These premises were linked by a small canal to the River Suir. The site of the mill in Portlaw was also particularly attractive. With a natural fall on the river of over 14 feet it could provide the power to turn the water wheel that would power the mill. The final factor in the establishment of a cotton mill was the influence of James Cropper, a Quaker from Liverpool who visited Ireland during this period. Cropper argued that mills would provide the masses in Ireland with work and would thereby improve their lot. As a Quaker, David Malcomson now had a solution that met both his business needs and his religious ethos. Until its

406. The Square, Portlaw c.1910.

closure in 1876, the cotton mill would become the focal point around which the village developed and prospered.

Work began almost immediately, and it was reported that in 1825 over 100 masons and labourers were employed on the site. The first phase of the factory complex consisted of six storeys and thirteen bays. The main spinning building was 260 feet long, 47 feet wide and 72 feet high. An additional thirteen bays connected by two link bays were constructed between 1837 and 1839. By 1846 the total investment was reported as being more than £100,000, which equates to approximately €11.5 million in today's money. The total number employed was in excess of 1,000 by this period. Some of the earliest workers were brought from Lancashire and the northeast of Ireland. These skilled workers trained the locals in the manufacture of cotton.

The new mill prompted a spate of building and renovations, most of which were linked to the Malcomsons. Some of the first housing developments built by the Malcomsons were English Row, the Ivy Walk and Green Island. These houses no longer exist although the site of the Green Island houses is visible from the village. English Row was a terrace of fifteen stone-built, slate-roofed houses along with a community hall. This hall also functioned as a mechanics lecture room, a reading room, a temperance lecture hall and a Methodist place of worship. These houses were mainly the residences of skilled workers from the cotton mill and were of a high quality. The Ivy Walk was a row of six superior-quality houses located on the edge of the factory premises. Close to the Ivy Walk was Mayfield House, the Malcomson

family residence, described in 1850 as one of the finest houses in the county. The other significant housing development was Green Island which consisted of fifty-seven houses. These were stone-built, slate-roofed dwellings finished with lime mortar, located on the island between the river and the canal. For the rest of the workers the two principal streets were the parallel terraced houses that made up Shamrock Street (forty-six houses) and Mulgrave Street (forty-seven houses). These houses were probably typical of their time – small, mud- and stone-walled with thatched roofs. Other significant developments were Curtis Street with eighteen houses and Thomas Street with forty-six houses; the Thomas Street houses were of a lower standard and were reported as being in poor condition in 1848. The row of houses along what is now known as Brown Street, many of which were owned by the Medlycotts, took its form from a pre-existing route linking the Mayfield House area with the Carrick Road.

One of the visible anomalies of Portlaw is that the police barracks and the Catholic church are situated well outside the centre of the village. The reason for this is that the original village was located around the church: it consisted of roughly seventy labourer's cottages. The police barracks was located close to these cottages. All these houses were vacated by 1830 and their residents moved over to the new village.

Water was one of the key resources that made Portlaw attractive to David Malcomson. Between 1825 and 1830, a canal was built connecting the River Clodiagh and the factory complex to transport raw materials in and finished goods out by barge. A significant proportion of this raw cotton originated in North America. It was shipped to Liverpool and then Waterford before being transported to Portlaw by barge.

The water from the river powered two large overshot wheels which generated 160 hp and a smaller wheel which generated 40 hp. Supplementing this power were steam engines capable of generating 120 hp. This was important during the summer months when the river levels were low, as steam would supplement water power. By 1850 the combined horsepower for water and steam had reached 500. A large mill pond of approximately three and a half acres was supplied by water running from the River Clodiagh at the north end of the mill and provided a vast reservoir for the plant. Water and steam provided the energy to power the large weaving sheds, large foundry and workshops which sustained the business.

The Malcomsons were often praised by factory inspectors for their efforts to provide a safe working environment for their employees. There is an account in the *Waterford Mail* of 25 August 1857 which relates the visit of the Lord Lieutenant to the Mayfield Factory and Schools:

His Excellency and the Marquis of Waterford were first conducted to the offices of the firm, and afterwards through the mechanics, fitting, and turning departments; next proceeded through the carding, spinning, winding rooms, etc, etc ... [His Excellency] expressed himself highly pleased with the neatness, style, and order in which those extensive premises are kept.

However, the equipment was dangerous and accidents still occurred. People worked on average between twelve and thirteen hours a day with a half-day on Saturday. Deaths were commonplace, both from physical injury and illness caused by the dusty, unpleasant working conditions and exposure to chemicals.

Of great historical significance is the social aspect of the Malcomsons' Quaker ideals and how they impacted on the life of the village. Dr James Martin was employed by the Malcomsons in 1835 as resident surgeon. Together they focused on the social conditions of the society which surrounded them. The Mayfield Provident Society was a system of social insurance for workers who became ill, but workers lost eligibility for benefits if their illness was brought on by 'drunkenness, debauchery, rioting, quarreling, or playing unlawful games on the Sabbath'. The system was unusual in 19th-century Ireland. Workers under fifty years of age were eligible for the scheme and were entitled to cash benefits on becoming ill. In 1838 the Tontine Club, which had strict rules, was formed to promote temperance. The club also doubled as a savings scheme into which members paid sixpence a week, with the capital and interest paid to the members at the end of the year. However, if you were caught frequenting alehouses within a certain radius of the village or under the influence of drink, your savings were forfeit. The politician Richard Lalor Sheil wrote of his friend David Malcomson:

Originally he employed Englishmen; but he found that the Irish on being properly instructed were just as expert. The English had intermarried with the families in the vicinity and a perfectly good understanding prevailed, which had never been deviated from. The strictest morality was preserved and it was the rule to dismiss any girl who was guilty of the slightest impropriety.

407. The cotton mill (left) and Mayfield House (right) with the mill pond in the foreground c.1910.

Drunkenness had been banished and a school had been established where no sectarian animosities, no quarrels about the Bible were allowed to prevail. Here all the children of the factory were instructed in reading, writing and the elements of arithmetic, and no sort of interference with their religion was attempted.

The Malcomsons implemented a system of fines for minor infractions of factory rules in preference to outright dismissal which would have had a more substantial impact on the worker. The fines were paid into the factory poor box.

There is no doubt that Portlaw survived the worst ravages of the Famine due to the presence of the cotton mill, the attitude of the Quakers towards charitable works and the philanthropic efforts of the Marchioness of Waterford. An article appeared in the *Waterford News* in early 1846 on landlord absenteeism and noted that Portlaw was well cared for by Lady Waterford. The Malcomsons, like many other Quakers, were deeply committed to famine relief and were members of the Central Relief Committee of the Society of Friends. This was a national organisation set up by the Quakers in November 1846 to combat the worst effects of the Famine in Ireland. The committee imported food and clothing from Quakers abroad and set up soup kitchens to feed the poor. They also engaged in long-term projects such as grant-aiding the distribution of seeds and teaching new agricultural skills. The *Waterford Chronicle* of 7 January 1847 reported that:

the Malcolmsons do not get enough credit when compared to the Marquis of Waterford who expends approximately £200 a week to labourers and into the community while the

Messrs. Malcomson and Shaw pay weekly in leather tokens the sum of £500 which has kept the people of Portlaw comfortable.

A submission to the Boundary Commission in 1850 appears to support this view. The submission relates to proposed changes in electoral division boundaries and states:

of the 63 persons at present in the Union Workhouse from Portlaw Electoral Division four only were ever in factory employment, which, contrasted with the large number in constant work (over 1,400), fully bears out the statement that the factory operatives and their dependents have other sources than the poor rates in times of difficulty.

The submission goes on to state that the workers never received as much as dispensary aid as the cotton mill supported a medical establishment of its own.

In Portlaw during the Famine there were two types of resident. An influx of desperate souls from the surrounding area moved into the poorer-grade housing, while the mill workers were relatively protected from the ravages of the Famine. There were many reports of road construction and repairs to existing roads in the locality. These were public works carried out as part of part of an outdoor relief programme designed to provide employment to an increasingly desperate people. The year known as Black '47 saw a couple of interesting reports in the newspapers which showed the differences between those supported by the Malcomsons and those who didn't enjoy such aid. The *Waterford Mail* of 31 March 1847 reported:

About two o'clock on Wednesday evening two

cars of flour were attacked at Ballydine by two armed men, disguised; they took away six sacks from the carman, Patt Fleming, of Portlaw, where he was taking it to the Messrs. Malcomson and Brothers, from Clonmel. The police from Carrick turned out on hearing of the outrage, but got no trace of the offenders, or flour.

On 1 December 1847 the same paper highlighted that '[t]he Marquis of Waterford, we are glad to learn, is now employing from seven to eight hundred men, in building four miles of a wall on his estate at Curraghmore'.

The seventh report of the Irish Poor Law Commissioners outlined the costs and numbers of temporary fever hospitals in Ireland. It shows that a fever hospital was established in Portlaw, which would appear to have been a substantial undertaking based on the net amount (£492) advanced for its running (to contextualise this, the corresponding amount for Cashel, a much larger town, was £386). The date of requisition for the fever hospital was 17 March 1847. During the first half of 1849 a serious outbreak of cholera reached Waterford having swept across Europe, adding its own grim number to the death toll. While Waterford city, Lismore and Dungarvan had a mortality rate of over 50% among those who contracted the disease, Portlaw only had a mortality rate of 18% which corresponded to thirteen deaths. *The Abstract Return of Medical Establishments under Poor Law in Ireland* (1850) shows that the temporary fever hospital at Portlaw, used during the cholera epidemic in June and July 1849, was vacant the following year.

During the Famine the 1848 Young Irelander rebellion took place. There are detailed accounts of Lord Waterford travelling from Curraghmore to Waterford for arms and ammunition. The main house was secured, barricades put in place and special constables sworn in. A large force of rebels arrived in Portlaw on 15 September 1848. In the resulting siege of the police barracks one rebel was shot dead, another was fatally wounded and a third received wounds to his lungs from which he later recovered. The arrival of troops from Waterford forced the rebels to disperse and, apart from the energetic pursuit of the rebels, the attack was over. In the aftermath of the rebellion a new police barracks was built with the support of Lord Waterford to house a greater number of constables. Lord Waterford saw the benefits of the construction in terms of protecting his own house. The old barracks was renovated to accommodate an officer. The constables lived above the stables and in the barracks. It is said that the architect was William Tinsley and folklore has it that the design was intended for use in India. The building has the appearance of a small fortress with loopholes and fortified entrances.

The second phase of housing development began in the 1850s and continued into the late 1860s. This development was driven by several factors which included the deteriorating quality of the existing housing and the philosophy of William Malcomson who was by now the senior partner in the business. William had strong views on the care of workers for whom he felt he had a moral responsibility. He was also aware of the benefits that caring for a workforce could bring to a business. This view had emerged amongst some industrialists, many of whom were engaged in cotton production, from about the beginning of the 19th century. They intended to create villages for their workforce with houses constructed to a high standard, supported by robust infrastructure, schools and healthcare.

Portlaw has a unique streetscape with a Baroque layout of triangular blocks of housing leading to an open space and then directly to the factory gates. Three house types were built: two different two-storey designs and a single-storey design. The quality of the housing was far superior to the first phase of village housing and reflected the progressive thinking of the day. There is no doubt but that the influence of Dr Martin is reflected in the design. The rooms were 11 feet high and very airy, which was considered healthy. Each house had a range in the kitchen and a privy (toilet). A unique feature of the range was a tank which was added to the side, in which water could be heated providing hot water for cleaning and washing. Water was available from public pumps located

in the streets; pumps were fed from the pond in Milford House. Rent collection also played a role in maintaining good living conditions. Instead of deducting rent from wages, the Malcomsons employed a rent collector who also monitored the condition of the houses. Any instances of lapses in hygiene standards were reported to the factory surgeon.

One of the striking architectural features of the houses is their distinctive roof design, known as the Portlaw Roof. The roof was spanned by light curved lattice trusses made from memel pine to a standard specification. This in turn was spanned by layers of tar and calico. Calico came from the cotton-weaving process; the tar was a by-product of the gas works supplying the factory and village. The exterior of each building was decorated with a distinctive bargeboard. What was unique about these roofs is that everything used was manufactured

408. The Copper Lodge at Milford House c.1900. The name was derived from the copper roof.

in the factory locally at a fraction of what it would have cost if it was sourced elsewhere. Many of these roofs survived up to the late 20th century. Interestingly, the Malcomson's enterprises in the Ruhr Valley in Germany included coal mines and examples of these roofs can also be found in the mining town of Gelsenkirchen.

Many other buildings were built in Portlaw during the mid-19th century. These included major houses such as Woodlock, Milford House and Clodiagh House along with civic buildings such as the courthouse and school. Other structures built during this period included the Church of Ireland Holy Trinity Church and St Patrick's Catholic church. The present St Patrick's Church was built in 1858 on the site of a smaller cruciform church. An article published in the the Dublin Builder newspaper on 1 May 1859 describes the work:

A new Catholic Church in the early Gothic style from designs by J.J. McCarthy, R.H.A. has just been roofed in Portlaw, Co. Waterford. It consists of chancel, nave and aisle, with bell turret and porches, sacristy and spire are yet to be built. The Church is 110ft. long and 60ft. wide in the clear. The aisle walls are 14ft. and the nave walls are 34ft. high, height from floor to nave ridge 60ft. The chancel is separated from the nave by a lofty arch 42ft. high. The aisles are lit by single and double light windows, and the clevestory by 10 spherico triangular lights. A lanceloted triplet gives light to the Sanctuary; and in the western end is a window of two-light, with masonry mullion and traceried top. The roof is open to be stained and varnished hereafter. The leaden sashes and ventilators are set in from granite, of which material all the dressings are comprised. The walling is faced with dressed limestone in horizontal and perpendicular joints, which has a very pretty effect. The work was commenced in April 1858 and the whole shell was completely covered in the short space of 10 months. The expenditure was about £2,500. The builder was Mr. Richard Pierce of Wexford.

James Joseph McCarthy was a talented architect and an able administrator who designed many churches and cathedrals including St Patrick's Cathedral, Armagh, St Patrick's College Chapel, Maynooth, Ss Quan and Brogán, Clonea, and Holy Cross, Tramore.

One distinctive feature of Portlaw life in the Malcomson era was the 'leather money' or 'cardboard tokens' which were used as currency in the village shops. This practice began in 1834 with two-shilling tokens, followed by one-shilling and fourpence tokens. These tokens were used to pay the workforce and could be used in the Mayfield Stores to purchase goods at favourable prices. When most people hear of this system it evokes negative images of the 'company store' exploiting workers; however, the opposite was the case. One of the reasons put forward for their use was that it was dangerous to transport large amounts of money to pay the workers. This did not stop negative commentary and there was a well-publicised libel action in 1844 when accounts were carried in two Dublin newspapers attacking the token system:

We are informed of one factory in this country of which the Quakers are proprietors, where no money at all passes from the tyrant to the slave: but where small tokens of stamped leather (cardboard) procure goods at the shops of the tyrants, which on this trick system, they impose at their own profit on their miserable slaves; this we believe to be entirely illegal and it certainly is wholly unconscientious.

The Malcomsons were awarded £500 in damages.

The cotton mill suffered several hammer blows which eventually led to the demise of the business. The American Civil War resulted in a significant decline in the supply of raw cotton. The Malcomsons' bank, Overend, Gurney & Co., collapsed with significant losses for the family, and the withdrawal of substantial shareholdings by Joseph Malcomson's widow combined with this to undermine the business. The factory closed in 1876 and the village's population dropped from over 4,500 to just over 1,100 in the 1901 census as many of the skilled workers emigrated to find work. A good proportion of the workers moved to the mill towns of England but also further afield. This population drop resulted in a change to the built landscape of the village. Many of the vacant houses fell into disrepair and contemporary accounts paint a bleak picture of the

village. The mill staggered on until 1904 in the form of the Mayfield Spinning Company which was run by William and Joseph Malcomson (sons of William, the last chairman). It had a staff of about 100 before it too collapsed.

Like many other communities across the Ireland, Portlaw was strongly impacted by World War I. Over seventy local men served in the trenches and twenty-five women served at home with the Red Cross or in military hospitals as nurses. While estimates vary, approximately 200,000 Irishmen from north and south are thought to have fought in the war. Many of those from Portlaw and other parts of Ireland who participated in the early stages of the war were regulars or reservists. As noted above, Portlaw at the beginning of the 20th century was a village in decline. There was very little employment other than at Curraghmore and one can surmise with a high level of confidence that many of the men enlisted for economic reasons. The remainder would have joined the new divisions raised in the immediate aftermath of the outbreak of hostilities. The 10th Irish

409. Portlaw 'leather money' or 'cardboard tokens', used as currency in the village shops.

was formed in late August 1914 and the 16th Irish in September 1914. Portlaw men are listed in the rolls of honour of eight of the nine Irish infantry regiments in the British Army in 1914. Sadly, more than thirty of the men from Portlaw paid the ultimate price. Those who survived returned to a changed country. Many of these ex-soldiers never mentioned their experiences and banished their memories to the furthest recesses of their minds.

The 20th-century industrial story of Portlaw has some parallels with the 19th-century development of the cotton mill. After five decades of neglect, which saw the population fall by almost 75% and parts of the housing stock fall into disuse, redemption came in the 1930s. The Free State government established protectionist policies aimed at protecting existing domestic employment and promoting employment initiatives. This led to the establishment of the Portlaw Tannery by Irish Tanners Ltd on the old cotton mill site in the early 1930s, led by managing director and principal shareholder Kennedy O'Brien. The tannery was officially opened by the Minister for Industry and Commerce, Seán Lemass, in 1935. A 1937 newspaper article about the tannery provides a postscript to the era of the cotton mill:

an old man of 94 applied for work in the tannery, said he had been a Malcomson employee, and asserted his name should be first on the pay-roll. Every Saturday he stands outside the paymaster's office, as if unwilling to believe he has not been included in the latest development...

Empty houses were reoccupied and over the next few decades new houses were built to house the workers as many of the old workers' homes were now derelict.

By 1937 the tannery was processing over 3,000 hides per week. A lot of alterations were made to the original mill. A massive new purpose-built

410. John Joy's grocery, drapery and butcher's shop, Portlaw c.1910.

concrete structure was added in 1945. Tanning had a long history in Ireland and has been described as one of the oldest manufacturing industries, but like many other traditional industries it faced commercial challenges. In the early 1950s, sole leather plants were closing all over the world as the competition from cheaper rubber soles grew. To survive, the company diversified its operations. Along with finished leather uppers and suede in the main plant, the short-lived Leather Board was started in 1956 but was destroyed by fire shortly afterwards. Waterford Rubber and Plastics was set up in 1958 and operated until the closure of the plant. Another subsidiary, Protein Foods, processed waste fleshings from the limeyard – these were used in the production of dog meal. Animal fat was extracted and used in the production of soap and candles. Along with many other manufacturing industries the tannery suffered during the recession of the 1980s. It finally closed its gates in 1985 after a long and painful process of rationalisation and layoffs, like so many other manufacturing companies of the period the victim of global competition.

For the second time in just over a century, Portlaw was in decline. The village struggled for a period following this but is now developing steadily as a satellite town for Waterford city. While the building of council houses has changed the streetscape somewhat, there are enough of the original workers' houses surviving to give an idea of how the village looked in the past. Despite Portlaw's rural setting, the people of the village have been deeply influenced by their industrial past. Slowly, recommendations from the heritage conservation plan for Portlaw are being implemented. Portlaw continues to evolve, looking to the future while always conscious of its past.

410. Irish Tanners factory, Portlaw c.1950.

N

Curraghmore House

Cotton Mill / Tannery

RIVER CLODIAGH

Holy Trinity
Church of Ireland

MAIN STREET

PORTLAW
HERITAGE
CENTRE

Caldbeck
Memorial Fountain

Portlaw

0   100   200   300   400m

411. *Map of Portlaw.*

412. The abandoned Portlaw tannery in 2018.

413. Curraghmore House.

Cotton mill/tannery

This nationally important industrial heritage complex was originally established as a cotton mill, forming the centre of a planned village founded by David Malcomson in 1825. The construction of the cotton mill ranks in scale with the great industrial sites of England and North America. The site is of importance historically for having supported the economy of Portlaw. It was converted in the late 19th century into a spinning factory and later a tannery in the 1930s. Although now inaccessible and in a dilapidated condition, interesting technical and engineering features survive intact.

Curraghmore House and demesne

Curraghmore House is a Classical-style house with an impressive forecourt. The house is the centrepiece of a planned demesne which has been continuously developed by the Power (le Poer) family since the 15th century. The estate consists of 2,500 acres of woodland, grazing fields and formal gardens making it the largest private demesne in Ireland. The gardens include an arboretum, a Japanese garden and the Shell House, a folly created by Catherine, Countess of Tyrone in 1754.
See www.curraghmorehouse.ie.

Portlaw Heritage Centre

This house is a former Malcomson building and was used as a dispensary. It has been home to the Portlaw Heritage Centre since 2005. The building demonstrates an architectural feature unique to Portlaw, the Portlaw Roof, which consists of curved trellised softwood frames covered with layers of tarred calico cloth to form a semi-flat roof. The centre provides a focal point for the preservation and conservation of the industrial, social and cultural history of Portlaw. See www.portlawheritage.ie.

St Patrick's Catholic church

A Gothic Revival church, built by Richard Pierce to designs prepared by James Joseph McCarthy (1817-82). The church interior contains a variety of items of artistic interest, including fine timber joinery, stained-glass panels, and an exposed timber roof construction. The adjacent graveyard includes a number of gravestones that display high-quality artistry and craftsmanship.

Holy Trinity Church of Ireland church

This church was built in 1851 in a Gothic Revival style to designs prepared by William Tinsley. Interesting architectural details include distinctive Hindu-Gothic-style motifs. The construction of the church involved high-quality local stone masonry using red and yellow sandstone. The church interior is distinctive for its stained glass panels, decorative carved stonework and fine timber joinery including the exposed timber roof.

Clonegam Church of Ireland church

Situated in the grounds of Curraghmore demesne, this church was built in 1741, renovated in 1791, and restored in 2001. It is of interest for its fine cut stone, demonstrating a high quality of masonry and craftsmanship. It contains some impressive monuments of the Beresford family, besides some 18th-century stained glass panels. A white marble monument depicting a reclining woman and her baby (1873) is a splendid example of the work of the noted sculptor Sir Joseph Edgar Boehm; it was commissioned by the 5th Marquess in memory of his first wife, Florence Grosvenor Rowley, who died in childbirth. The surrounding graveyard, which is centuries older than the church, has many finely carved headstones and table tombs commemorating local families of c 1750 to c 1950.

Presbyterian church and manse

This fine building was dedicated to the use of the local Presbyterian community - mainly tenants and employees on the Curraghmore estate - in 1845 (the date over the tower door). The records, now held in Belfast, record baptisms between 1843 and 1909. The adjacent building is the former manse, the residence of the local minister.

Kilbunny Church

The church of St Munna was built around the 8th century and is noted for its 11th-century Irish-Romanesque doorway. Near the door arch is a stone carved with the head of a lion. There are two bullaun stones outside the doorway and an altar built into the eastern wall. An effigy of

414. Holy Trinity Church.

415. Portlaw village c.1910.

416. Clonegam Church, built in 1741 and restored in 2001.

a bishop with the inscription 'S. Monnia Episcops', a 17th-century grave cover and two quern stones from the site are now in the National Museum of Ireland.

Clodiagh House

Clodiagh House was built in 1863 for Frederick Malcomson to designs prepared by John Skipton Mulvany (1813-70). Distinctive architectural features of this building include the veranda, window openings, rendered dressings and profiled timber joinery. The structure has been renovated in recent years by the Health Service and functions as a community hub.

Mercy Convent

This building was constructed in 1810 and has historic associations with the Malcomsons. The house was acquired as a residence for a foreman and was thereafter intended to be developed as a railway station. It was subsequently converted to a convent in 1883. The chapel is a later addition, built by J.J. Healy to designs prepared by J.R. Boyd Barrett, with funds provided by Dr Jeremiah Kinane, Catholic Bishop of Waterford and Lismore.

Almshouse

The centrepiece of a terrace of seven houses is a three-bay, single-storey, gable-fronted stone almshouse, dated 1896, incorporating the fabric of an earlier house built c.1860. It was originally a 'Portlaw'-type house having a shallow segmental barrel roof. The building was renovated to demonstrate the benevolence of the Marquess of Waterford.

Le Poer Tower

Le Poer Tower stands on an elevated site overlooking Curraghmore demesne and was built by George de la Poer Beresford, Earl of Tyrone (1735-1800) in 1785. The view from the tower is picturesque and the inscription on the tower reads: 'Le Poer Tower, erected in the year 1785 by George, Earl of Tyrone, to his beloved son, his niece and friend'.

Royal Irish Constabulary barracks

Built to designs prepared by William Tinsley (1804-85), this building is distinguished by a number of features, including corner towers and slit-style gun loop openings, giving it a medieval, fortified appearance. According to the National Inventory of Architectural Heritage, the barracks, 'together with the attendant officer's house, is of

417. Portlaw Presbyterian church, built in 1820.

418. *Royal Irish Constabulary barracks, built after the rebellion of 1848.*

particular importance as one of the earliest purpose-built civic buildings in the locality'.

Woodlock House

An imposing Classical-style mansion, Woodlock House (also known as Portlaw House) was built to designs prepared by John Skipton Mulvany between 1861 and 1864. The house shares design elements common to several Malcomson properties, including a bow-ended wing that also features at Mayfield House and Villa Marina in Dunmore East. The house has been extensively renovated following its acquisition by an international internet publishing company.

Courthouse and school

This Classical-style building, combining a courthouse and school, was built in 1845 to designs prepared by John Skipton Mulvany. The building is of significance having been sponsored by the Malcomson family as one of the earliest structures forming the civic centre of the planned model village of Portlaw. The shell of the building still exists and retains some important features, including the remains of the distinctive Portlaw Roof.

Mayfield House and gate lodge

Mayfield House was modified in the 1850s for the Malcomson family to designs prepared by John Skipton Mulvany. The house is noted for its elegant entrance tower and the Italianate Classical quality of its design. The Italianate gate lodge was probably designed by Mulvany to complement Mayfield House. The gateway to the east was designed by Richard Turner and made at his Hammersmith Ironworks in Ballsbridge, Dublin, and reflects a Mulvany style. Two flanking double gates were operated by

a chain mechanism that is of technical and engineering interest. According to the National Inventory of Architectural Heritage, '[t]he gates and railings are fine examples of early mass-produced cast ironwork'. These are in a poor state of repair.

Martin Hospital

The Martin Hospital was a retirement home for the elderly. It is named after Dr James Martin who served as a resident surgeon in the Mayfield Cotton Factory from 1835 to 1890. Dr Martin was also responsible for at least one major archaeological find at Kilbunny Church. The present building, which is on the site of the old fever hospital, is now a day care centre providing services for the older residents of the area.

419. Woodlock House, built between 1861 and 1864.

420. Mayfield House, the Malcomson family residence. In 1850 it was described as one of the finest houses in Co. Waterford.

Caldbeck Memorial Fountain

This fountain occupies a prominent site in the centre of Portlaw, forming the focal point of the Square. The fountain is named after prominent local postmaster and shopkeeper William Robert Caldbeck (d. 1887). Although local tradition states that the fountain was cast in the Mayfield Foundry, this is unlikely, as it is a custom design produced at the Saracen Foundry in Glasgow. It was probably shipped unassembled, to be constructed and customised in the local Portlaw foundry.

Mount Congreve

The Congreve name derives from Congreve in Staffordshire which was the family's principal seat from the 14th century. The family has produced some notable people, including poet and dramatist William Congreve, Sir William Congreve, 1st Bart, who made improvements to the manufacture of gunpowder, and his son William, 2nd Bart, inventor of the Congreve rocket, Congreve clock and much else.

The first of the family to settle in Waterford was the Revd John Congreve who died

421. Mount Congreve, built c.1760.

in 1710. His son Ambrose played a leading part in the affairs of Waterford city and served as mayor in 1736-7. He was the first of three generations of the family to represent Waterford in the Irish Parliament. He died in 1741 leaving a son and heir, John, who married Mary Ussher of Kilmeaden. In 1759 John Congreve acquired the lease of a property belonging to the Christmas family of Whitfield, and the following year he built a Palladian-style house there called Mount Congreve, designed by the noted Waterford architect John Roberts.

During the Civil War in 1922 the house was occupied by members of the anti-Treaty IRA, led by George Lennon. Mount Congreve was inherited by Ambrose Congreve (1907-2011), son of Major John and Irene Congreve. Ambrose Congreve took over the running of the estate in 1968. He made radical alterations to the 18th-century house, removing the fine cut-stone portico and adding an extra storey to the single-storey side wings. Regrettably, he also removed the early 18th-century canvas paintings of mythological figures by Willem Van der Hagen which once hung on the dining room walls.

The highlight of Mount Congreve is the garden created by Ambrose Congreve from the 1950s onwards. It comprises about seventy acres of intensively planted woodland garden and a four-acre walled garden. The garden was awarded the Veitch Memorial Medal by the Royal Horticultural Society in 1987 and a gold medal by the Horticultural Society of Massachusetts in 2001; the latter society classified it as a 'Great Garden of the World'. The garden is now open to visitors on a regular basis. See www.mountcongreve.com.

Further reading

Desmond G. Neill, Portlaw: *A nineteenth-century Quaker enterprise based on a model village* (1992), ISBN 0-9519870-2-X

Tom Hunt, *Portlaw, County Waterford, 1825-1876: Portrait of an industrial village and its cotton industry* (2000), ISBN 0-7165-2722-7

Bill Irish, *Shipbuilding in Waterford, 1820–1882: A historical, technical and pictorial study* (2001), ISBN 1-869857-50-X

WATERFORD

Ireland's oldest city, founded by Vikings in the 10th century.

I was a day in Waterford,
There was wine and punch on the table.
There was the full of the house of women
there,
And myself drinking their health.

Port Láirge
(translation of traditional Irish song)

Come with me to Waterford to sing and
make merry.

On the capture of the O'Driscoll chief
in Baltimore, Co. Cork by Mayor Simon
Wickens, 1413

The story of Waterford begins in the Viking Age, that turbulent period of raiding and gradual integration that stretched from the 9th to the 11th centuries. The Vikings first arrived in Ireland in 795 and in subsequent centuries established what are now the island's oldest towns and cities. West of present-day Waterford city, near Carriganore on the banks of the River Suir, a recent archaeological excavation uncovered a settlement named Woodstown which sheds further light on the foundation and development of Waterford. Over the course of the excavation, over 6,000 artefacts were uncovered from a double-D or B-shaped enclosure. It is believed that Viking raiders occupied Woodstown from around 832 to 848.

However, the settlement declined over time. The historian Clare Downham argues that 'the present site of Waterford may have been more easily defended … Waterford was closer to the estuaries of the Barrow and Nore … Waterford may have provided a better location for a quay than Woodstown'. Woodstown and its findings demonstrate that Waterford history is ever-evolving: new information and interpretations are continually changing the narrative. On the 400 metres by 60 metres of the site that has been excavated, finds include balance-weights, a pagan-warrior burial and a 9th-century silver coin of Arab origin known as a Kufic dirham.

Vedrafjordr: Viking Waterford

It is difficult to precisely date the foundation of Waterford. Originally a Viking settlement called Vedrafjordr (meaning the fjord of castrated rams or windy fjord) was in existence by 914. This Norse name is the origin of the modern name 'Waterford'. It is Ireland's oldest centre of continuous urban settlement and the only Irish city to retain its old Norse-origin place name and is older than most northern European capitals (with the exception of London and Paris). It remained Ireland's second city (behind Dublin) until the end of the 17th century. In 917 a Viking, Ragnall, took control of the city while the native Irish (who called the area Port Láirge) led by Niall of the Black Knee attempted to rid Ireland of the Norsemen. A three-year siege did little to further this. Ragnall became King of York in 918 after defeating the Scots by the River Tyne and thus King of Waterford and York. His descendants ruled Waterford, Dublin and York until 952.

Another foundation story is that Waterford was established by a Viking chieftain named Sitric in 853. Gerald of Wales, writing in the 12th century, states that three brothers, Amalavus, Sitricus and Ivarus settled in Ireland and respectively created the cities of Dublin,

Waterford and Limerick. Meanwhile, the 13th-century biography of Welsh king Gruffudd ap Cynan records that the Norwegian king Harald Finehair established Dublin and gave Waterford to his brother, whose descendants continued to rule the city.

The Irish name for Waterford, Port Láirge, translates to 'port of a thigh'. One explanation for the name comes from the *Táin Bó Cúailnge (The Cattle Raid of Cooley*, the most famous tale in Irish mythology) which recounts how the Brown Bull overpowered his adversary Findbennach, whose thigh-bone was thrown to Port Láirge. Another explanation comes from the pre-11th-century book *Dindshenchas Érenn* which tells of a young prince named Rot who dies at sea, torn apart by sirens, leading to his thigh-bone being washed ashore at Port Láirge. Yet from 915 to 918, the alternative name for the area was Loch dá Chaech, meaning 'the lake of the two blind people'; it is subsequently referred to as Waterford harbour.

502. Reginald's Tower.

Vedrafjordr was a triangular settlement, established on a tidal inlet at the confluence of the the Suir and St John's River. The area was safeguarded by a fort named Dundory (believed to have stood near where Reginald's Tower is today). Whatever protection this offered, it did not prevent the city from being destroyed four times (in 1031, 1037, 1088 and 1111). The Viking territory had three main streets: High Street formed the hub of commercial activity, while four smaller streets cut across these larger ones. Over the course of archaeological excavations in the 1980s and 1990s, the remains of seventy-two sub-rectangular houses were uncovered dating to the 11th and 12th centuries, constructed with wattle-and-daub walls and thatched roofs.

In 1996, archaeologist Orla Scully uncovered the timber floor of a Viking Age ship while excavating a quay wall on the Mall beside City Hall.

The elevation of the Uí Briain (O'Brien) family to power in Munster led them to rule Waterford from 976. The city was the meeting place in 984 for King of Munster (and later High King of Ireland) Brian Boru and the sons of Aralt, the Norse King of Limerick. Brian sought a Limerick fleet to aid his attack on Dublin, which finally took place in 1014 at Clontarf where he received support from the Hiberno-Norse of Limerick and Waterford. Although Brian died in the battle, the Waterford faction defeated one of the rivals to the high kingship in the person of Máel Sechnaill. The Waterford historian Eamonn McEneaney notes that '[t]his defeat highlights the importance of the port towns in Irish politics and the close relationship existing between the native population and the descendants

of the original Viking settlers'.

By the 11th century, Waterford was beginning to transfer allegiance from the kingdom of Munster to Leinster when in 1037 it was seized by Diarmait mac Máel na mBó, King of Uí Cheinnselaig (Kinsella), with coins later being minted in the city under his sponsorship. On his death in 1072, Waterford came under the control of Munster, when Brian Boru's grandson Toirdelbach took command of Leinster. He was succeeded in 1086 by his son Muirchertach who reigned as High King from 1093 to 1114, becoming the most dominant king of Ireland. He installed his brother Diarmait as ruler of Waterford in 1096, the same year that the Ostmen of Waterford sought a bishop to lead their clergy who worshipped at buildings such as St Olaf's. (Ostmen were people of mixed Gaelic and Norse ancestry and culture.) Malchus became Waterford's first bishop and brought liturgical practices in line with those of mainland Europe over the course of his forty-year episcopacy.

Previously, in 1088, Waterford had been unsuccessfully attacked by a rival to the King of Leinster. It remained under the influence of Muirchertach Ua Briain until he was deposed by his brother Diarmait in 1114 who ruled until his death four years later. It is unclear who succeeded Diarmait as ruler but by 1137 Waterford was defended by King Cormac Mac Cárthaigh (McCarthy) of Desmond when attacked by Diarmait Mac Murchada of Leinster and Conchobar Ua Briain of Thomond. Around the time of the attack the city's defences on the western side were strengthened with a stone wall replacing the timber palisade. Waterford remained under Mac Cárthaigh rule until 1170 when it was captured by the Anglo-

Normans, after a siege led by Raymond le Gros.

In return for Anglo-Norman mercenaries to help him regain his lost kingdom, the King of Leinster had promised the marcher lord Richard de Clare, better known as Strongbow, his daughter Aoife in marriage. Strongbow's side of the bargain fulfilled, the wedding ceremony took place at Christ Church in Waterford, thus signalling the end of the Viking Age in Ireland. The following year upon the death of Diarmait Mac Murchada, Henry II, King of England arrived in Waterford, Diarmait Mac Cárthaigh submitting to Henry in the city he once ruled. McEneaney writes:

[i]t is ironic that the Vikings, founders of Ireland's first towns, with their expertise in naval matters and improved weapons technology, should turn out to act as catalyst for the development of a more centralised Ireland, making it possible for the Anglo-Normans to achieve a foothold over a major part of the island in the decades after 1170.

The first frog discovered in Ireland was found in a grassy meadow near Waterford and was believed to have been brought here among the baggage of Strongbow's mercenaries during the Anglo-Norman invasion.

A royal city: Anglo-Norman Waterford

From the arrival of the Anglo-Normans in 1170 a century of economic and political progress began which saw Waterford take advantage of its proximity as a port to Europe and Bristol (one of the most important ports in medieval England) for trade. King Henry II created

503. Cattle fair at Ballybricken, 4 May 1910.

the groundwork of administrative infrastructure by making Waterford a royal city. By landing at Waterford, Henry II became the first English king to set foot in Ireland.

The Ostmen were expelled and settled outside the city in the area now known as Ballybricken. This 'Ostmantown' subsequently became the Anglo-Norman extension of Waterford. Ballybricken predates this extension to around the 1170s while the late-12th-century developments by the Anglo-Normans were ad hoc compared to the structured layout of Viking Waterford. The city's quays were not expanded as part of the extension due in part to new merchants seeking to maintain control of the port.

Medieval kings granted charters which gave settlements and their inhabitants the right to town privileges under the feudal system. These charters allowed wealthy merchant families to conduct the internal affairs of the city. This led to trade being top of the agenda for Waterford. Charters conferred on Waterford include the charter of 1215 by King John which saw elected representatives of the city's merchants gain command of the courts. Previously, King John had allowed the city to hold an annual fair during the first

504. Arundel Square, Waterford c.1900.

eight days of August, which attracted foreign merchants to the city. Around 1195-6 the monarch established a mint at Reginald's Tower which was then closed in 1204 (on the creation of the annual fair) and reopened in 1210.

Under King John the city's original defences were strengthened while three new stone gates were constructed before 1212. They were named Arundell Gate, Colbeck Gate and St Martin's Gate. Reginald's Tower was rebuilt and the Anglo-Normans expanded the city westward with the development of Barronstrand Street and John's Street. Waterford adopted the irregular narrow streets and laneways typical of the medieval period.

The streets had to connect to the gateways of the city. Ballybricken was thus joined by the creation of Patrick Street (those travelling from the north of the city would have to cross the Suir and enter Waterford from Ballybricken) and John's Hill and Johnstown to the south (entering the city via John's Bridge). Broad Street became the centre of commerce in the Anglo-Norman expansion. Michael Street and Stephen Street also date from the 13th and 14th centuries. It appears that the expanded area of Waterford acted as a separate entity with the city walls signifying and reinforcing a sense of distinction between the Viking triangle and the Anglo-Norman suburb.

The high point came in 1272 when Waterford was given the right to elect a mayor. Prior to this development, Waterford paid a fixed sum of 100 marks to the king, then the second highest rent paid by an Irish city. The mayor was then personally responsible for the debts of the city which had to be accounted for annually to the Exchequer. Successive monarchs upheld Waterford's claim that all foreign ships entering the city must dock at Waterford harbour instead of New Ross, promoting the city's continued prosperity and importance. Waterford was also designated a wine port. In 1232 King Henry III conferred the right of having to pay only half the tax paid by other ports. This made the city the medieval wine capital of Ireland.

In 1281 the mint was re-established in Waterford with Mayor Roger de Lom as its keeper. It closed the following year but reopened twelve years later under the tutelage of the appropriately named Roger the Goldsmith. Some of the Waterford merchants to share in the city's prosperity included Frenchman Eymar de Godar of Gascony, a four-time mayor of the city, and Italian Servasius Copale who worked as a customs official in the city.

Waterford also had a substantial interest in the wool and hide trade. The introduction of the Great New Custom (a tax on such goods by King Edward I to fund his campaign against the Scots), generated around one fifth of the total revenues for the Anglo-Norman colony in Ireland. Such tax was used to fund the defence of the city, which by the end of the 13th century was surrounded by walls. The Middle Ages saw many churches and monasteries built in the city. Again, King John looked favourably on Waterford by endowing Christ Church Cathedral, constructed in the Gothic style beginning in 1210. The arrival of the Dominican and Franciscan religious orders to the city reinforces the

505. *A view of Waterford city c.1746.*

505. *A view of Waterford city c.1746.*

505. A view of Waterford city c.1746.

505. A view of Waterford city c.1746.

idea that Waterford was embracing the religious movements developing across Europe. The Franciscans established their friary around 1240 (financed by Sir Hugh Purcell) and it became known as Greyfriars as the friars wore habits made from grey cloth.

The devotional practices of the Middle Ages are reflected in the naming of streets. In the Viking settlement of Waterford, we have streets such Peter's Street (after St Peter's Church), Lady Lane (after the Church of Our Lady) and Olaf's Street (after St Olaf's Church) while the Anglo-Norman streets of John, Michael and Stephen are all named after churches or other places of worship in those locations.

The Black Death arrived in Ireland in 1349 and saw nearly one third of Waterford's population of 3,000 die of bubonic plague. This was followed by a decline in local trade which led the merchants of the city to develop trade with Europe. A further impact of the plague was that the city did not expand beyond the 13th-century city walls.

In the 1370s, as part of a dispute with the neighbouring port of New Ross, an important legal document was created. Trying to maintain Waterford's status as an influential port city, the Great Charter Roll, a compilation of previous charters and documents from 1215, was put together. It was illuminated with illustrations of several Kings of England. Waterford was looking to demonstrate loyalty to the English crown. It was a last-ditch effort in trying to prolong the city's golden age which was now coming to an end. This is reflected further in the earliest use of English in official Irish documents being found in Waterford's

Great Parchment Book (1360-1649).

Urbs Intacta Manet Waterfordia: Late Medieval Waterford

Waterford [with] *no more than seven acres of land within its walls is like a little castle.*

Petition to King Edward III from Mayor William Lombard, 1371

Waterford continued to struggle to regain the prosperity it had enjoyed in the 13th and early 14th centuries because of the impact on trade made by the Hundred Years' War between England and France. King Richard II sought to maintain Waterford as a royal stronghold against the McMurroughs of Wicklow by beginning an expedition to Ireland in the city in 1394. Richard's court (a gathering of the extended royal household) was held at Greyfriars where the Irish princes submitted to his rule. Local governance was carried on with a fair degree of independence, due in part to the weakness of the Dublin government. This continued into the reign of Henry IV with special provisions for the mayor of the city.

New Street and New Gate were developed around the 15th century leading out to the area where modern-day Barrack Street is located. The later medieval city was around 53 acres in circumference. A guesstimate of Waterford's population at this time would be around 5,000 people.

By the middle of the 15th century Waterford's defences included twenty-three towers and fifteen gateways. McEneaney notes:

cities like Waterford provided the facilities to

exchange agricultural produce for luxuries and imported necessities. The 14th- and 15th-century wars in which the city had been embroiled were not wars of conquest but attempts to extract protection money and it would be safe to assume that many of the disputes arose when the city refused to pay up or when extra money [was] *demanded.*

Two of Waterford's long-time foes in these wars were the Powers of Dunhill and the O'Driscolls, a piratical family whose home port was Baltimore. In 1461, at a battle near Ballymacaw, the Waterford forces captured the O'Driscolls' leaders and three of their galleys. It is believed that these are the three ships that feature on the Waterford coat of arms. The mayoralty was further strengthened by local legislation recorded in the Great Parchment Book. When Edward IV ascended to the throne he issued a charter further strengthening the relationship between Waterford and the crown. An upturn in the wool trade led to growth and investment in local monasteries with the addition of bell towers to both the Franciscan and Dominican churches in the latter half of the 15th century.

In 1463 the Irish Parliament met at Waterford and after a break of almost two centuries a mint was re-established at Reginald's Tower. One of the key figures in the affairs of the city was James Rice. Mayor of Waterford on eleven occasions, he worked in the best interests of the city and had an inclusive style of governance. His cadaver tomb in Christ Church Cathedral is one of the finest examples of an Irish 'apostle tomb'. In 1483 a rule was passed by the corporation that parents would be held responsible if their children broke the glass windows of churches, an illustration

of the esteem in which the Church was held at that time.

Waterford further demonstrated its loyalty to the English crown when it refused to accept the pretender Lambert Simnel to the throne of Henry VII in 1487. In 1495 the city was unsuccessfully besieged by the forces of another pretender to the English throne, Perkin Warbeck. In the first use of artillery in the siege of an Irish city, cannons from Reginald's Tower sank one of Warbeck's ships during the eleven-day siege. In recognising the city's steadfast loyalty to the king, Henry VII gave Waterford the motto *Urbs Intacta Manet Waterfordia* – the city of Waterford remains untaken.

Parva Roma – little Rome: 16th- and 17th-century Waterford

The city of Waterford much flourisheth, and I suppose was never in better estate since it was builded, the people thereof very civil and (for this country) full of industry.

Sir Henry Sidney, Lord Deputy of Ireland (1567)

The Gentle Shure, which passing sweet Clonmel, Adorns rich Waterford.

William Spenser, *The Faerie Queene* (1590)

Waterford is situated upon the best harbour and her beauty is in the Quay.

Luke Gernon, Second Justice of Munster (1620)

Henry VII granted the city a charter in 1510 which contains the earliest acknowledged image of Waterford city's coat of arms. The dissolution of the monasteries and the English Reformation brought the Franciscan friary at Greyfriars

WATERFORD

1745

→ THE RIVE

	15 The Mall	44 Georges Key	
	16 The Bowling Green	45 Christ Church &yard	
	17 Brick Lane	46 St Oliver's Church	
1 Barron Strand street	18 St Francis Lane	31 The Corrigeen	47 St Peter's	60 Guild Hall
2 Broad Street	19 X Church Lane	32 Alexander Lane	48 St Michael's	61 Blew Boys School
3 Michael Street	20 Goose Gate Lane	33 St Johns Lane	49 St Johns	62 Mc Masons School
4 Johns Street	21 Kempsons Lane	34 Bowling Green Lane	50 St Stephen's	63 Black Fryars
5 Big Patricks Street	22 Old Corn Market	35 The Rampart	51 St Patrick's	64 French Ch Holy ghost ho
6 Stephen's Street	23 Conduit Lane	36 The Mayors Walk	52 The Barracks	65 Mc Congrevs Dock
7 New Street	24 Chappel Lane	37 The Fair Place	53 Patrick's Gate	66 The Leper house
8 Litle Patricks street	25 Balys Lane	38 The New Road	54 New gate	67 King Street
9 High Street	26 Lady Lane	39 The New Road	55 Johns Gate & Bridge	68 Lombard Street
10 Peters Street	27 Bakehouse or litle Lady lane	40 Spring Ally	56 Cole Peck Gate	69 The Apartment
11 Litle Barron Strand st	28 Arundel Street	41 Batchelors Walk	57 Bishop's Palace	70 St Mary's Lane
12 David Balys new street	29 The Square	42 Cole Peck Lane	58 The Exchange	71 The Ring Tower
13 Georges Street	30 Norningtons Lane	43 St Catherinas Abby	59 The Custom house	72 St Thomas Chappel
14 Hanover Street				73 The Fish house

Pomarede Sculpt

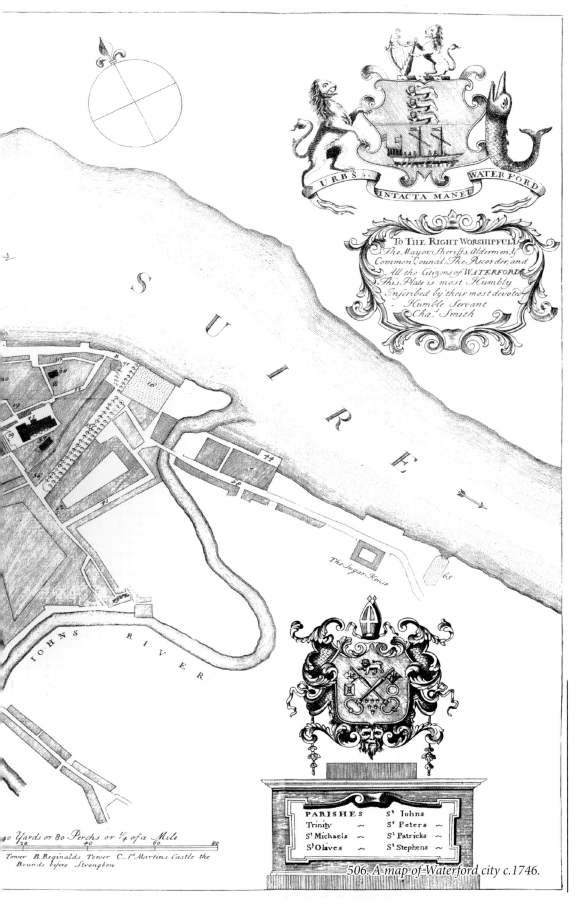

URBS WATERFORD

INTACTA MANET

To The Right Worshipfull The Mayor, Sheriffs, Aldermen, & Common Counal, The Recorder, and All the Citizens of WATERFORD This Plate is most Humbly Inscribed by their most devoted Humble Servant Cha.' Smith

S U I R E

The Sugar House   65

IOHNS RIVER

40 Yards or 80 Perchs or ¼ of a Mile
20   40   60   80

Tower B. Reginalds Tower C. S.' Martins Castle the Bounds before Strongbow

PARISHES	St Iohns
Trinity ~	St Peters ~
St Michaels ~	St Patricks ~
St Olaves ~	St Stephens ~

506. A map of Waterford city c.1746.

under the ownership of the local Walsh family. In 1544 the friary was converted to an almshouse named the Holy Ghost Hospital. With the Reformation, many of Waterford's churches and monasteries were destroyed and many of their great treasures were lost forever. Although many wealthy families such as the Walshes acceded to Henry VIII's Act of Supremacy (acknowledging the king as the head of the Church), they cherished the old Catholic traditions by saving religious statues that had previously decorated local churches.

Waterford's golden age came to an end in part because of the decline in the power of the Anglo-Norman lords and the heavy taxation policies of Edward I. There was little improvement in the city's fortunes under the reign of Edward II with the rival Power family of Dunhill laying waste much of the countryside outside the city walls.

Under Henry VIII the city's defences were reinforced for the first time since the 13th century. Don Diego Ortiz, a Spanish spy who visited Waterford in 1574, recorded that 'the city contains nearly a thousand houses. It is surrounded by a stone wall, something less than a mile in circumference, with seventeen towers, and cannon on them to keep off savages. It is the richest town in Ireland after Dublin'.

The city was struggling to remain within its confines though the dissolution of the monasteries may have freed up space for further development. The building of larger timber-frame houses in the 16th and 17th centuries within the 13th-century city walls was becoming increasingly difficult.

Waterford's loyalty to the crown was unquestioned until the reign of Elizabeth I and the reforms she sought to establish in the church. The city's ability to trade with continental Europe had led to the local merchants developing a faithfulness to Rome and the Catholic Church. The government strengthened the city defences with the construction of St Patrick's Fort outside the city walls to control passage on the River Suir. A map dating from the late 16th century shows the stone wall of the city stretching from Reginald's Tower towards the south-east and a blockhouse in front of the tower for cannon.

During the Nine Years' War (1593-1603) Waterford was the landing point for government forces. In 1598 Sir Henry Norreys arrived in the city with 2,000 soldiers before besieging the town of Cahir in Co. Tipperary. The billeting of such large numbers of soldiers in the area was considered a factor in the spread of plague, with 256 deaths being recorded for the year ending September 1604 alone.

The death of Queen Elizabeth I was hailed in Waterford as a return to Catholic practices with the clergy prematurely taking control of the cathedral and churches that had been given over to the Protestants. However, the Dublin government made sure that the Protestant status quo that characterized Elizabeth's reign remained. Waterford continued to refuse the Oath of Supremacy to King James on religious grounds, resulting in the local government of the city being suspended in 1618. The charters of the city were taken to Dublin and for the rest of James' reign Waterford was ruled by government officials.

The Irish Confederate Wars, also called the Eleven Years' War, took place between 1641 and 1653. The conflict initially pitted native Irish Catholics against English and Scottish Protestant colonists. It ended with Royalists, Irish Catholics and Scottish Presbyterians fighting the ultimate winners, the English Parliament. During the war, Waterford supported the Confederate Catholics of Ireland. The outbreak of the war in 1641 led Waterford to permit the Catholic Confederate army of Lord Mountgarret within its confines and Waterford remained in Confederate hands until 1650 when the city finally fell to the army of the English Parliament. Around this time, in a letter to prominent Franciscan friar and historian Luke Wadding, Waterford is referred to as *Parva Roma*, little Rome, because of its loyalty to the Catholic Church and the large number of influential Catholic scholars from the city, including Wadding himself.

Cromwell reached the outskirts of the city on 24 November 1649, commencing a siege which lasted nine days. The siege was lifted due to bad weather, lack of artillery and an outbreak of dysentery in the Parliamentary camp. Waterford eventually surrendered to Cromwell's son-in-law Henry Ireton in August 1650. A cannonball from this siege is still lodged in the wall of Reginald's Tower. Many Catholics were subsequently dispossessed of their lands, some being transported as indentured servants to Barbados. A largely Protestant corporation was formed which attempted to keep Catholics on the periphery of the city's governance.

In the latter years of the reign of Charles II, several Catholics were granted the status of freemen of Waterford which allowed them to operate as merchants. A silversmith, Edmund Russell, was commissioned by the corporation to make copper tokens to be used within the city. Upon James II's accession to the throne in 1685, Waterford was granted a new charter which allowed the corporation to elect representatives to Parliament in Westminster. A Catholic majority of the corporation came into being in the latter half of the 17th century but the renaissance for Catholics in the city was interrupted in July 1690 when Waterford surrendered to the Protestant King William of Orange. The city's inhabitants were granted sympathetic provisions in response to their prompt submission. Waterford Corporation did not have a Catholic member among its assembly again until the mid-19th century with Thomas Wyse.

A map of Waterford dated 1673 shows some development in the vicinity of modern-day Catherine Street and Johnstown but this was limited in scope.

The crystal city:
18th-century Waterford

...many of the private buildings of the City are sufficiently handsome and spacious, but several of the streets and lanes are for the most part exceedingly narrow, and the houses crowded very thick together, yet were the streets more open, and having houses that lie thick set, ranged in a regular order, the City would take up three times the ground that it does at present.

Charles Smith, 18th-century historian

Over the course of the 18th century, Waterford was transformed from a walled territory to a modern European city. Medieval defences were removed and medieval churches were altered in accordance with contemporary architectural fashions. The city's expansion was aided by the diversion of St John's River and the development of a new suburb named Newtown. *Waterford treasures* (2004) outlines that 'almost ninety per cent of buildings of historic and architectural interest either date from the late 12th-13th centuries or the 18th century'. The demolition of the internal city walls took place in the 1690s while the removal of the city gates began in 1695. The wall which lined the quayside was removed in the 18th century, as was the artillery blockhouse adjacent to Reginald's Tower in 1711. Today, six of the city's towers remain, including Reginald's Tower, the French Tower and the Watch Tower. Along the Quay the construction began of three- and four-storey, red-brick, gabled-fronted houses in the 'Dutch Billy' style. The quays were then linked to Ballybricken with the creation of King Street (now a part of present-day O'Connell Street), Hanover Street and New Road (now Thomas Street) by 1764. The street names reflect the desire of the governing Protestant minority in Waterford to demonstrate their loyalty to England and the crown.

With the Protestant Ascendancy in control of the Dublin Parliament, many Catholic families from Waterford migrated to the Continent (particularly

THE BRIDGE, WATERFORD.

507. Redmond Bridge c.1949.

France and Spain), due to the limitations placed on them by the Penal Laws. These laws were passed to limit the religious, political and economic activities of Catholics. Catholics who remained in Waterford were prohibited from holding public office although some were made freemen. By the mid-18th century the city's population included Baptists, Presbyterians and Quakers. A period of prosperity led to street lights being installed in 1732. The Mall was designed and constructed in the same decade once St John's River had been diverted. The historian Charles Smith described the Mall in 1746 as:

a beautiful walk, about 200 yards long and proportionably broad ... it is planted with rows of Elms, and the sides of the walks are fenced with a stone wall ... Here the Ladies and Gentlemen assemble on fine evenings where they have the opportunity of each other's conversation. Nothing can be more agreeable than to see this shady walk crowded with the fair sex of the City, taking the air, enjoying the charms of a pleasant evening, and improving their healths...

Such was the wealth of the city that the corporation commissioned the artist Willem Van der Hagen to produce the painting 'View of Waterford' for £20 in 1736; this is said to be one of the oldest detailed views of its kind of an Irish city.

As the third-best-connected port in 18th-century Ireland, Waterford traded with 400 ports across Britain, mainland Europe, Scandinavia, North America and Newfoundland. Central to the city's trade were commodities such as salted beef, pork and butter. By 1770, fifty ships, primarily owned by Catholic merchants, called Waterford their home port. Waterford-Newfoundland was one of the important trade routes. Seasonal migration for work in the cod fishing industry led around 33,000 people from Waterford and its environs to settle there well into the early decades of the 19th century.

Further architectural developments included the construction of the present Bishop's Palace and the refurbishment of Christ Church Cathedral. The late 18th century saw an improvement in relations between Catholics and Protestants. The Catholic Relief Act of 1793 permitted Catholics to have the same rights as Protestants in relation to voting in parliamentary elections. However, Catholics could still not become members of parliament. The city can claim to be the first place in the British Isles where a Catholic cathedral was built after the Reformation. Furthermore, it was the Protestant architect John Roberts who was commissioned to design it. Roberts left the greatest mark in terms of the most important civic and cultural buildings in Waterford. He has the distinction of being the only man to design both the Protestant and Catholic cathedrals of a northern Europe city. This led the architectural historian Edward McParland to write in 1985:

Waterford more than any other city in the country in the late 18th century succeeded in expressing its civic dignity with fitting architectural grandeur ... The density and quality of building in Waterford, however, made the city architecturally pre-eminent. No city of its size had, within its boundaries, as grand a bishop's palace. No 18th-century cathedral elsewhere in the country – with the possible exception of Cashel – outdid either of John Roberts's two Waterford cathedrals.

By 1784, a Wide Streets Commission

8. 'View of Waterford' by Willem Van der Hagen (1736), one of the oldest detailed views of an Irish city.

had been created, which led to the broadening of Barronstrand Street, and the removal of Little Barronstrand Street, Garter Lane and Royal Oak Lane to produce an open area north of Broad Street. In addition, the Apple Market by John Street was created by demolishing a block of buildings. The infrastructural development of the city was further aided by the construction of the first bridge across the River Suir in 1794. The builder was an American, Lemuel Cox, and the total cost came to £14,000. This wooden toll bridge was colloquially known as Timbertoes and was the city's main bridge until 1913 when it was replaced by the John Redmond Bridge.

In the words of local architect Michael Fewer, the development of a bridge aided the cause of Waterford's 'prominent citizens to have the city realise its full economic potential, to climb out of the Middle Ages and become integrated with the rest of Ireland. A substantial bridge spanning the Suir was for them the keystone of this policy'.

Some of the leading figures in Waterford during the 18th century were Quakers (accounting for 2% of the city's population), including brothers George and William Penrose who established the Penrose glass factory in 1783, which remained in operation until 1851. Two notable pieces created by this factory include the chandeliers of City Hall and a wine decanter dated 1789 which is now housed in the Bishop's Palace Museum.

19th-century Waterford

The view of Waterford, from the opposite side of the river, is very handsome, from a fine Quay nearly a mile in length, which runs along the river side, the whole extent of the city, the buildings on which fronting the river, a distance of the breadth of a moderate street are very good; also from a greater number of steeples and towers, than are able to be seen in most other towns, of the same size, in Ireland. There has been erected, a few years ago, a long wooden bridge across the great river Suire at Waterford by Cox, the famous American Bridge maker.

John Gough, *A Tour of Ireland* (1817)

Presently we caught sight of the valley through which the Suire flows, and descended the hill towards it, and went over the thundering old wooden bridge to Waterford. The view of the town, from the bridge and the heights above it, is very imposing; as is the river both ways. Very large vessels sail up, almost to the doors of the houses, and the quays are flanked by tall red warehouses, that look at a distance as if the world of business might be doing within them.

William Makepeace Thackeray, *Irish Sketch Book* (1842)

Waterford's trading connections with Newfoundland continued and from 1809 to 1815 there was increased movement of people and commodities (primarily cod). The conclusion of the Napoleonic Wars led to a decline in the economy and trade. One man to prosper despite the economic downturn was Thomas Meagher, originally from Newfoundland, who resided with his wife Alicia in a Georgian house on the Quay (where the Granville Hotel now stands). The building was subsequently leased to the Italian carriage entrepreneur Charles Bianconi who adapted it as a stagecoach station. The Meaghers eventually moved to a property at 19 The Mall named Derrynane House (after the birthplace of Daniel O'Connell). Waterford was sympathetic to the cause of O'Connell and Catholic Emancipation.

The momentum from the successful Catholic Emancipation movement led to a campaign for repeal of the Acts of Union between Britain and Ireland. Meagher became the first Catholic Mayor of Waterford in well over a century. The Repeal movement received financial support from the Irish diaspora in Newfoundland. The second Catholic to be elected to Parliament in London was Waterford-born Thomas Wyse (in 1830 representing Tipperary). Wyse broke away from the Repeal movement and became influential in educational reform, helping to create the National School system.

Another reformer who made a huge impact on the education of the poor was Edmund Rice, originally from Callan in Co. Kilkenny. He established the Christian Brothers religious order and founded his first school in Waterford, named Mount Sion, in 1802. This educational movement spread across Ireland and the world in the years that followed.

In 1820, Henry Denny invented the bacon rasher by sandwiching long, flat pieces of meat in dry salt. This led to the bacon lasting longer and revolutionised the meat industry. Another major Waterford contribution to the food industry was the opening of the biscuit factory in November 1850 by W.R. Jacob, a Quaker. In 1885 he invented the cream cracker at his bakery on Bridge Street. His company subsequently invented the fig roll in 1903.

509. Adair's Bakehouse, 18 Lady Lane c.1896.

510 The Thomas Francis Meagher Bridge

The blaa, a doughy, white bread roll is another food speciality particularly associated with Waterford. The blaa was reputedly brought to Waterford in the 17th century by French Protestant refugees know as Huguenots. The name is believed to be derived from *blanc*, the French for 'white', due to the flour sprinkled on top. The European Commission has awarded the terms 'Waterford Blaa' and 'Blaa' a Protected Designation of Origin (PDO).

Migration continued between Waterford and Newfoundland, allowing for individuals to improve their social status while providing employment opportunities. This has been cited as one of the reasons why the Great Famine was not as damaging to Waterford city as to the rest of the country. Poverty was still a feature of city life: Scottish travel writer Henry D. Inglis described in 1834 how he 'visited some of the worst quarters of the town, and was introduced to scenes of most appalling misery'. As the wealthier classes left the city centre to live in mansions outside Waterford's confines, the Georgian houses they emptied became slums. This led to overcrowding which was worsened when people from rural areas sought relief in the city. Such poor conditions contributed to an outbreak of cholera in 1832.

To combat cholera, the corporation sought to build new sewers, widen streets and improve the city's water supply. The latter half of the 19th century saw the corporation's first housing scheme at Green Street where seventeen two-storey houses were constructed in 1878-9.

An outsider's view of 19th-century Waterford comes from Johann Georg Kohl from Bremen, who travelled across Ireland in 1842, the English translation of his narrative being published the following year. He illustrates his first view of the city thus: '[w]e soon after beheld the valley of the Suir, the lofty picturesque shore of rock on both its sides, and the beautifully situated town of Waterford, like a pearl in its mouth'. Kohl notes that Waterford was at that time Ireland's sixth largest city with a population of 30,000 inhabitants at the start of the decade. In 1821, the population was recorded as 28,676 and by 1831 had increased by just 145 people. However, this small population growth did not slow the growth of trade in Waterford: exports doubled, with grain being the main product shipped.

During the Famine, a workhouse was established on John's Hill to provide relief for the struggling population. *An introduction to the architectural heritage of County Waterford* states that 'Waterford city hosted the greatest variety and number of substantial public buildings, including those built for the welfare of others [in Co. Waterford in the 19th century]'. By March 1847 there were 1,063 people in the Waterford workhouse. In the summer of the same year fever was at its worst, leading to a temporary fever hospital being established in the city. A major impact of *An Gorta Mór* (the Great Hunger, as the Famine was known) was the decline in the population of Ireland from death and emigration. Waterford being a substantial urban area, many people were attracted from more destitute rural areas in search of relief. In 1841, the population of the city stood at 23,216, rising to 25,297 by 1851. The 1850s saw continued migration as the population of the entire county of Waterford declined.

Political life continued despite the unfolding tragedy of the Famine. The above-mentioned Thomas Meagher's son, Thomas Francis Meagher, broke away from O'Connell's campaign for repeal of the Union. As a part of the Young Ireland movement he advocated the use of physical force in achieving independence from Britain. His speech at Conciliation Hall in Dublin on 28 July 1846 gained him prominence within the Irish Nationalist movement. Thomas Francis Meagher first flew the Irish tricolour (designed and presented to him by a group of French women) from 33 The Mall in 1848, the same year that the Young Irelander Rebellion took place. He went on to become one of the city's most famous sons, fighting in the American Civil War and later becoming Acting Governor of Montana. He disappeared in 1867 and is believed to have drowned in the Missouri River. Meagher wrote of his native city:

Waterford never appeared to me to change. For a century at least, it has not gained a wrinkle nor lost a smile. In every season, and for a thousand seasons, it has been and will be the same old tree. If no fresh leaf springs, no dead leaf drops from it. The Danes planted it; Strongbow put his name and that of Eva, his Irish bride, deep into its bark; and King John held court beneath its boughs; James the Second hid his crown into the crevices of its roots, and fled from it to France. It has witnessed many other events; many other familiarities have been taken with it. Many worse blows have been given it, since the Earl of Pembroke hacked it

511. Waterford port c.1890.

with his sword. But it has suffered nothing. *The dews, and the storms, and the frost, and the summer heat, have come and pass away, hurting nothing; improving nothing; leaving it, at the end of ages, the same old dusty, quiet, hearty, bounteous, venerable tree. Heaven bless it! And may the sweet birds long fill its shady trellises with music; and the noble stream with full breast nourish the earth where it has root!*

Shipbuilding in Waterford

The growth of steamships in the 19th century saw a revival of shipbuilding in Waterford. The first recorded steamship on the River Suir was the *Princess Charlotte* in June 1817. (The *Princess Charlotte* was built by the Clyde Shipping Company in 1814.) By the late 19th century, five in six ships in use across the world were built in the United Kingdom of Great Britain and Ireland. This level of production was reflected on the Waterford quays.

On the Ferrybank side of the river, Whites and Pope and Co. were in operation during the 1820s. Up to 1865, there were four shipyards (three in operation simultaneously) building sixty vessels in total. One of these was the Penrose shipyard located by the pier head next to the flour mills.

Some notable ships made in Waterford include the *Pathfinder* constructed by the Charles Smith shipyard, launched on 1 May 1858 and used primarily in the copper ore trade on the west coast of South America. The most renowned ship manufactured by the Pope and Co. shipyard was the SS *Kilkenny*, built in 1837. It was subsequently purchased by the East India Company and renamed *Zenobia*. Waterford maritime historian Bill Irish writes of the *Zenobia* that it

'was one of the first steamships to make the passage around the Cape of Good Hope to India'. By 1841, Waterford and Cork accounted for 41% of ships built in Ireland.

The Neptune Ironworks were originally established as a repair yard for the ships of Joseph Malcomson Brothers in 1843. Four years later, the yard launched its own vessel, the SS *Neptune*, which became the first ship of its kind to regularly service the London-St Petersburg (Russia) route. On its first voyage up the Neva River the Neptune was met by Tsar Nicholas I on his royal barge, who ordered that whenever this ship was stationed at St Petersburg it did not have to pay its port tariffs. By the 1860s, the Neptune shipyard employed up to 400 workers with a new vessel being constructed every nine months on average. In 1882, they built the *Cella*, at the time the largest ship ever built in Ireland. Costing £33,500, it was later sold to owners in Constantinople (now Istanbul, Turkey) and renamed the *Sharki*. On the building of the *Cella*, an ordinary labourer earned ten shillings a week while a carpenter earned nearly three times as much. The last ship built by the yard was the steam yacht *Maritana*.

The world's oldest steamship company, the Clyde Shipping Company, began a weekly service to Cork and Waterford from Glasgow in 1859. Partnering with Malcomson Brothers, the Clyde operated a service from Waterford to London in 1870. Frank P. Murphy explains: 'the Clyde knew what they were up against and wisely co-operated rather than compete'. The demise of the Malcomsons' business led the Clyde to take control of the Waterford Steamship Company in 1912.

The First World War was a difficult time for the Clyde Shipping Company. A number of their ships were torpedoed during the conflict. The SS *Coningbeg* entered Liverpool on 26 April 1916 but was requisitioned to transport British Army troops to combat the Easter Rising in Dublin. The *Dunbrody* was also called into action in April of the following year when under the guidance of Captain Spillane she successfully rescued fifty-seven horses aboard the *Hermione*, which was torpedoed but managed to get near Waterford port. There was great tragedy in December 1917 when two of the Clyde's ships, the *Coningbeg* and *Formby*, were sunk by German submarine U-62 with the loss of eighty-three lives. After the war, the steamers of the Clyde were primarily used to transport cattle between Waterford and Liverpool. The last ship on this route, which ceased in 1968, was the *Rockabill.*

Midway through the 19th century, Waterford Corporation surmised that the future development of the city would occur at its western side, in the area now known as Gracedieu. The corporation believed that a sufficient public transport service was going to be central to aiding this development. In January 1878 it was agreed that a horse-drawn tram route be established with the construction of a double line tramway from Gilbert Hill (Gracedieu) to Adelphi Quay in the city centre.

The following month, the Harbour Commissioners made a submission to the corporation proposing that a tramway be developed connecting the railway system south of the River Suir to the port in order to aid trade. However, the Corporation were not willing to give any concrete promises to what appeared to be a potentially lucrative proposal. Albert Thornton notes that:

[t]*he proposed tramway was based on the premise that the Waterford, Dungarvan and Lismore Railway Company would provide a connection with the main railway network, by the construction of an extension railway from Waterford South Railway Station at Bilberry (Waterford Foundry Ltd), to a new city centre terminus at the junction of Bridge St. and Mary St.*

The line was given the go-ahead after an Act of Parliament for the development was passed on 22 July 1878. Unfortunately, the extension line was never built, and this subsequently hampered any future development of a tramway service in the city.

An unusual feature of political life in the city at the end of the 19th century was the Pig Buyers Association (1884-1935) based at Ballybricken. The Ballybricken pig buyers were recognised by John Redmond, MP for Waterford city and leader of the Irish Home Rule movement, for their 'patriotism and sterling spirit' in his electioneering in the 1890s. A trade disagreement occurred between the pig buyers and the bacon curers who sought to buy directly from farmers. This would have cut out the pig buyers, who acted as middlemen. It resulted in a violent economic blockade from 1892 until its climax in 1896-7 when the dispute was finally settled. Farmers seeking to sell to the bacon curers such as Denny's and Shaw's in Waterford city had to be escorted by police. At the height of the dispute 155 RIC officers were deployed, amounting to 'almost one for every pig buyer'.

Redmond played a pivotal role in

512. *Police patrol the streets during the Ballybricken Pig Buyers' strike c.1896.*

bringing the dispute to an end. He represented the pig buyers in court and gained favourable terms for the association, effectively returning the system of trade to its pre-strike state. Waterford labour historian Emmet O'Connor concludes that the outcome of the strike not only weakened the cause of trade unionism but strengthened 'working class conservatism' which helped to form 'the uniqueness of Ballybricken that underwrote the durability of Redmondism'. It was a political philosophy that continued into the 20th century.

20th-century Waterford

[The city's people are] ... *easy-going, light-hearted, frank, generous, but too much given to trivial amusements, and too apt to let things drift. They do not seem to think for themselves, and like to follow the example of their neighbour whether it be right or wrong.*

Report on the people of Waterford, *United Irishman* (1905)

The city has a noble position along its mile of quay, and there is a good hotel, the Imperial, at the end of the broad and dignified Mall which leads down to the quay.

Stephen Gwynn, *The Charm of Ireland* (1934)

In 1900, William Peare and Sir William Goff opened Ireland's first motor garage in Waterford city. It was a brand new, state-of-the-art premises on Catherine

Street with two storeys: the first floor was a space for offices and accommodation, with the ground floor acting as a workshop and showroom. Peare began to sell Gladiator cars in 1902, and later acquired the rights as an agent for Daimler, Oldsmobile, Napier, Buick and Cadillac. Sadly, the garage closed in 1917 as William Peare decided to join the army and fight in the First World War. Goff's role in the whole enterprise led to his Napier being the first registered car in Waterford, with the registration number WI 1.

King Edward VII visited Waterford in May 1904, knighting the mayor, James Power, as he departed the city from the train station at Bilberry.

John Redmond appeared to achieve his ambition of Home Rule for Ireland when the bill for a Dublin parliament was passed in 1912, to be enacted two years later. This was postponed due to the outbreak of the First World War. Redmond advocated Irishmen joining in what he regarded as a fight for the freedom of small nations. 1,756 Waterford city men enlisted in the British Army prior to 1916, 366 of whom died. The populations of the city and county at the time were 27,464 and 56,502 respectively. A disproportionate number of recruits and casualties came from Waterford city due to Redmond's strong support for the war.

The war brought economic benefit to Waterford with the export of cattle, increased demand in the bacon trade, the establishment of a munitions factory at Bilberry and almost full employment. Many prospered while the tragedy of

513. King Edward VII visits Waterford, 2 May 1904.

war unfolded. The historian Tom Hunt notes:

Ireland's commemoration of its war dead has always been compromised; at the war's end the country was on the verge of a revolution and those who returned from the war came back to a very different country. In recent times attitudes have changed...

In the 1918 general election Waterford city was the only constituency outside of Belfast to return a Home Rule MP, Captain Willie Redmond. Willie was the son of John Redmond who had died in March 1918. Willie Redmond's election was as much an endorsement of his father's legacy as a demonstration of support for any of his political ideologies.

During the War of Independence (1919-21), the East Waterford Brigade of the Irish Republican Army was one of the less active IRA units on the island. In their area, two members of the Royal Irish Constabulary, one civilian and four members of the IRA were fatalities during the struggle for independence. 1922 saw the outbreak of the Civil War after the ratification of the Anglo-Irish Treaty by Dáil Éireann. That July, some 300 members of the anti-Treaty IRA (also known as Irregulars or Republicans) under the command of Pax Whelan occupied public buildings in the city such as the Infantry and Artillery Barracks, the Jail, the Granville Hotel, the General Post Office and Reginald's Tower. Redmond Bridge was raised to prevent easy crossing of the River Suir. The Free State forces tried to regain control of the city, thus beginning the Siege of Waterford. These forces, led by Commandant-General John T. Prout and Commandants Heaslip and Paddy Paul (the latter of whom had commanded the East Waterford Brigade in the War of Independence), occupied Mount Misery

514. Redmond Bridge c.1915.

overlooking Waterford. With a single 18-pounder field gun they launched an attack on the occupied city.

On the night of 19-20 July, Free State forces slipped across the river and succeeded in taking some key buildings. The Republicans were forced to abandon successive outposts before finally abandoning the city and retreating westwards. On 21 July, three days after the siege began, Waterford city was finally brought under Free State control. Historian Michael Hopkinson notes that '[e]ven by the standards of the Civil War the fall of Waterford demonstrated an extreme unwillingness on the part of the Republicans to fight and a complete failure of co-operation between anti-Treaty forces'.

Over the years since the creation of the Irish Free State, which later became the Republic of Ireland, Waterford has like all Irish cities experienced economic booms and busts with the subsequent migration of its population across the globe. One of the most noteworthy stories of 20th-century Waterford concerns an immigrant who made the journey in the opposite direction. Glass manufacturing returned to Waterford after nearly a century when Waterford Glass was established by Czech glass manufacturer Karel Bacik in 1947. Born in Nová Říše in Bohemia, then a part of

515. The General Post Office, Waterford after bombardment by Free State forces, July 1922.

the Austro-Hungarian Empire, he left Czechoslovakia for Ireland when the Communists seized his glass factories. Waterford Crystal went on to become a major employer in the city for the rest of the 20th century, employing up to 4,000 people at its zenith.

Other important events that occurred in the 20th century include the construction, beginning in 1982, of Brother Edmund Ignatius Rice Bridge to replace the existing Redmond Bridge over the River Suir. The first homes in the city to have indoor toilets were built at St Carthage's Avenue in 1938. The most substantial public housing scheme in the city's history is St John's Park, constructed in the early 1950s. The first thirty homes here were reserved for Waterford Glass employees. Waterford Institute of Technology was established in 1970 as a Regional Technical College. A teaching hospital, Waterford Regional Hospital, was developed in 1987. It is now known as University Hospital Waterford.

Anthony Brophy's article 'How are we doing?' published in the *Munster Express* in 1999 highlights the following:

A leading historian has stated that geography governs history. Waterford helps prove the point and the portents are positive. Its location has always been at the business end of our overseas affairs. Ireland being a small and relatively remote island, access is vital. Since Irish history began Waterford Harbour has been pivotal to events shaping its early and medieval fortunes. Now, with Ireland's future bound more closely with mainland Europe, Waterford could not be in a better position. If the historian is right we are in pole position and the future – and thereby potential – is bright ... a fresher spirit abounds in contemporary Waterford

underpinned by a feeling that there will be success. We have in the past indulged in whipping ourselves with what might have been and look what others have achieved and casting blame all over the place. Now, there is more a feeling of determination to realise potential by persistent effort. There is no other way – geography will govern our future story only if we help it. We are well located – let's make sure we become well connected and in every sphere of local activity. Success will depend on us all – the blame game is over.

Into a new millennium and the fallout from the Celtic Tiger, 2000-14

Our city centre is where it was when Strongbow was a boy, Patrick Street is as steep today as it was when Columbus discovered America in 1492 and we still enter Waterford from the north via a bridge built on the same line as Timbertoes, which was under construction when Wolfe Tone was organising the United Irishmen in Belfast. Time has changed Urbs Intacta but the charm that a thousand years of history has brought is enduring.

Eamonn McEneaney

The 1990s saw major developments in the Irish economy, yet this appears to have led to little change in the landscape of Waterford city. Some changes included the creation of a nightclub quarter at John's Street, the construction of City Square Shopping Centre at Arundel Square and the pedestrianising of the city centre around what is now John Roberts Square. The construction of the Millennium Plaza yielded dividends with the hosting of the Tall Ships Race in 2005 (and again in 2011). David Toms considers these developments to have 'merely papered over the cracks of the effects of de-industrialisation and regional neglect' which were amplified with the subsequent collapse of the national economy in 2008-9. The closure of the Waterford Crystal site at Kilbarry was one of the major falls of an icon during the recession.

Yet renewal has come in the form of the Viking Triangle development and the House of Waterford Crystal on the Mall. It seems that promoting history and heritage has gone some way towards revitalising Waterford city.

Waterford is the fifth most populous city in the Republic of Ireland. The 2016 Census recorded the population of the city as 53,504.

516. The Quay, Waterford.

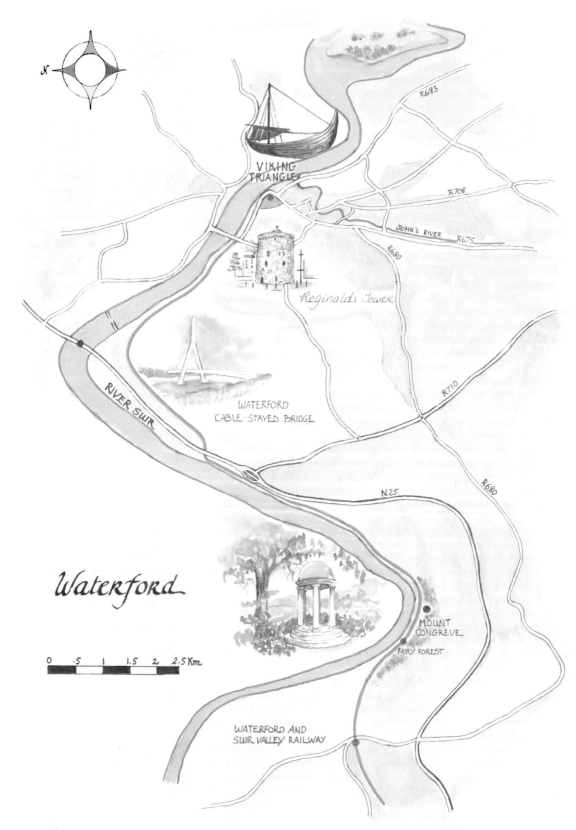

N

R683

R708

JOHN'S RIVER R675

R680

VIKING TRIANGLE

Reginalds Tower

R710

WATERFORD CABLE-STAYED BRIDGE

RIVER SUIR

N25

R680

Waterford

MOUNT CONGREVE

FAIRY FOREST

0   .5   1   1.5   2   2.5 Km

WATERFORD AND SUIR VALLEY RAILWAY

517. Map of Waterford.

The Quay

...indeed is not only the best and most convenient Quay which I found in Ireland, but it is as good a Quay as I have known either in England, or observed in all my travels...

Sir William Brereton (1635)

...unquestionably one of the very finest Quays I recollect to have seen ... The Quay of Waterford reminded me of the Quay of the Saone, at Lyons.

Henry D. Inglis, Scottish traveller (1834)

The Quay is the longest street in Waterford, stretching from Adelphi Lane to Bilberry Road. The earliest reference to the Quay is in 1377 when King Edward III granted the mayor and bailiffs of Waterford the cocket customs (customs duty) of the port for ten years. It seems the Quay was not fortified adequately (probably due to a failure to repair the city walls). The area was vulnerable to Spanish attack and the defences had to be improved. During the Middle Ages the south side of the River Suir, the 'Great Quay', was sandwiched between Turgesius' Tower (the area of Barronstrand Street) and Christ Church Lane (now Henrietta Street).

In the 16th century, the Great Quay was extended eastwards towards Reginald's Tower and by the latter half of the 17th century this area was set aside for the landing of timber. The quay and wall

518. Merchant's Quay, Waterford c.1890.

were ordered to be repaired by the corporation in 1674 and over the next couple of decades there were gradual improvements to the gates, docks and paving, culminating in a new extension from Barronstrand Street.

The Quay we are familiar with today is a result of the changes led by Mayor David Lewis in 1705. These included the demolition of the city wall which ran along the river. This was followed by further extensions to the west and east end of the quay. Such developments aided the growth and increased the affluence which the city experienced in the 18th century.

Waterford's prosperity in this period was due in part to the booming bacon and butter trade. Charles Smith recorded in 1746:

The Exchange, together with the Custom House adjoining are charmingly situated on the Kay. The Exchange is a neat light building, supported by pillars of hewn stone of the Tuscan order, the outside being adorned with the arms of the King, and those of the City, with an handsome clock. The roof is an Italian hipt roof, with a beautiful octogon cupulo, and a dome at top; the cupulo being surrounded by a balustrade, about which is a walk. The space below stairs for the merchants to assemble in, is sufficiently large and spacious, on one side whereof is the Town Clerk's Office, separated from the rest. Above stairs are the Council Chamber, and a large Assembly-room besides other apartments. In the Council Chamber is a

519. *Merchant's Quay, Waterford c.1963.*

very large perspective view of the City finely painted by Vanderhagen.

The New Quay was the site of the glass factory founded in 1783 by George and William Penrose with the assistance of a grant from the Irish Parliament. Also located on the Quay is the Granville Hotel, birthplace in 1823 of Irish nationalist and revolutionary Thomas Francis Meagher. The building was later obtained by Italian transport entrepreneur Charles Bianconi who converted it into a hotel and the Waterford terminus for his horse-drawn stagecoaches. Three years after Meagher's birth, the Quay was illuminated by gas lighting.

The year 1875 saw the commencement of construction of both the Custom House and General Post Office, the latter of which was expanded in 1883 to accommodate parcel post. Another extension of the Quay was completed by 1886 and stretched from the bridge to Strangman's brewery; it was named Grattan Quay. Other sections of the Quay include Adelphi Quay (between the Mall and the mouth of St John's River); Parade Quay (Keizer's Lane to Reginald's Tower); Custom House Quay (Exchange Street to Keizer's Lane); Coal Quay (Barronstrand Street to Exchange Street); Merchant's Quay (Bridge Street to Barronstrand Street); and Meagher's Quay (Gladstone Street to Conduit Lane).

In 1928 the Quay was surfaced with asphalt, the first time that a modern road-surfacing material was used in the city.

Clock Tower

One of Waterford's best-known landmarks, the Clock Tower on the Quay was built between 1854 and 1861 at a cost of £200. Designed by Charles Tarrant in the Gothic Revival style, the Clock Tower was constructed due to the boom in the shipping industry in Waterford and the importance of time to that endeavour. It has four cast-iron clock faces facing north, south, east and west with three drinking fountains (on the landward sides) providing fresh water for horses. The historian Julian Walton points out that 'the tower is a thing of beauty as well as of usefulness. Observe the fine quality of the stonework; the delicate spire; the diamond shapes and gothic pinnacles of the clock faces; the trefoil-headed recesses of the water stoups'.

Catholic Cathedral of the Most Holy Trinity

A very large Roman Catholic Chapel, or Cathedral, in this town. A light gallery affords the only fixed seats a remarkable feature in the Roman Catholic places of worship; and in which they have a great advantage over the Protestants, as to the true object of such buildings: all are open, and open alike to rich and poor: no appropriation of seats, or locked pews, or passport of money required. In this respect more appearance at least of devotion and spiritual service.

James Glassford, *Three Tours in Ireland, 1824-26* (1832)

Designed by John Roberts, the Classical-style Catholic cathedral was built in 1793 and is the focal point of Barronstrand Street. It is Ireland's oldest Catholic cathedral. Originally T-shaped, it was extended in 1829 with a the addition of a chancel to the east, and renovated in 1854. An Ionic limestone frontispiece was added to the entrance in the 1890s.

Inside, the cathedral has a tiled floor with carved timber pews, Corinthian columns and a timber panelled gallery to the first floor. The stained-glass windows were made by Mayer and Co. of Munich in 1885. The present organ dates from the 1850s and was built by William Hill and Sons of Liverpool at a cost of £1,700. It was played for the first time by W.T. Best on 29 August 1858. The cathedral was refurbished in 1977 after the Second Vatican Council with a new altar installed facing the congregation. There are ten Waterford Crystal chandeliers (gifted by the manufacturer) inside. The cathedral was refurbished again in 2006.

John Roberts Square

John Roberts Square was named in honour of the city's famous 18th-century architect in 2000, upon the completion of the pedestrianisation of Barronstrand Street. Prior to this the square was colloquially known as Red Square on account of its red paving stones (though some would suggest that the name was an allusion to Waterford as a 'hotbed of militant trade unionism'). Older generations referred to the area as the Cross on account of its triangular shape. The Waterford playwright Jim Nolan describes such vernacular terms as the 'poetry of the street'. The area is a popular meeting point with trees, sculpted seating and a modern pyramidal water fountain designed by the artist Eileen McDonagh.

Blackfriars Dominican priory

The only existing remains are the chancel of the church and the belfry. The entrance to the former is through an arched doorway, highly ornamented with rope mouldings and surmounted by a spacious window; the interior consists of two apartments, low and gloomy, with vaulted roofs supported on groined arches. The belfry is a lofty square tower of massive thickness, having a staircase leading to the summit, from which is obtained an interesting view, especially over the old portion of the city.

Samuel Lewis, *A Topographical Dictionary of Ireland* (1837)

Blackfriars is a Dominican priory built c.1230 between the old and new city walls. The shell of the church and tower survive today. The site was gifted to the order (who came here in 1226) by the citizens of Waterford. The name Blackfriars comes from the black *cappa* or cloak worn by the Dominicans. They established schools and educated the sons of the wealthy merchant classes in the city. The priory was dissolved by Henry VIII in 1540 and from 1617 was used as a courthouse, becoming a theatre in 1746.

William Vincent Wallace Plaza

Waterford's millennium project was opened in 2001 as the Millennium Plaza but was subsequently renamed in honour of the 19th-century opera composer William Vincent Wallace who was born at Colbeck Street in the city. His notable operas include *Maritana* and *Lurline*. Located in front of the Waterford Marina, the plaza has a permanent semi-oval dais to the west and wooden thrones covered by a canopy; the open space has wooden benches. There is a tall maritime-inspired sculpture designed by Liam Lavery which acts as a beacon for visiting ships and yachts. Its bow structure and the shields on the wooden thrones evoke the city's Viking past. A boardwalk connects the plaza with Rice

520. *William Vincent Wallace Plaza.*

Bridge at the other end of the Quay. The space hosts many public events, from art festivals to concerts.

Formby and Coningbeg Memorial

These two Waterford steamers were torpedoed between 15 and 17 December 1917 by the German submarine U-62 commanded by Ernst Hashagen. Both ships were lost with a combined crew of seventy-seven and six passengers all perishing at sea. Many of those who died were from Waterford city. The memorial to the victims was dedicated by President Mary Robinson in 1997.

Reginald's Tower

Reginald's tower – a massive hinge of stone connecting the two great outspread wings, *the Quay and the Mall, within which lay the body of the city.*

Thomas Francis Meagher

Reginald's Tower is Ireland's oldest civic building. It appears that the Vikings had a fortification at this location from the 10th century. The tower seems to be named after the the 10th-century Viking ruler of Waterford, Ragnall, or one of his successors of the same name. Built to defend entry to the city, the present tower was finished in two stages. The ground and first floor were built in the late 12th century while the upper floors were built in the 15th century (to accommodate the use of cannon).

The original entrance to the tower is at second-storey level. There are now two doorways at ground level, one of which led to the 16th-century blockhouse where cannon were kept. The present entrance was inserted into the tower in the 1590s to allow access to the blockhouse. The blockhouse was demolished in 1714. At the top of Reginald's Tower is a hole with a cannonball lodged in it. It dates from the siege of Waterford by the army of Oliver Cromwell in 1650 when ships on the River Suir bombarded the city with cannon fire.

The spiral stairs (known as stumble steps) are built into the walls of the tower. The steps are deliberately set at different heights to make them difficult for would-be attackers to climb. The fifty-six steps are orientated to the right to make it difficult for right-handed attackers to swing their swords. The walls on the ground floor of the tower are nearly 4 metres thick.

Over the centuries the tower was used as a prison, a mint and a defensive rampart. It was a prison from 1819 to 1850, primarily a lock-up for petty criminals and drunks. The last prisoner was Meg Collender who was sentenced to two weeks imprisonment for drunk and disorderly behaviour (a repeat offender who had committed the same offence 150 times). The top floor became known as the 'ballroom' as the female prisoners held there passed the time singing and dancing.

The tower then became the official residence of the High Constable of Waterford, the last of whom was James O'Mahony who died in Reginald's Tower in 1901. Today, it is a museum housing Viking artefacts from the Woodstown excavation. It is managed by the Office of Public Works.

Greyfriars Franciscan friary

In the Middle Ages, Waterford had a population of 3,000 with fifteen churches. Built in 1241, the Greyfriars Franciscan friary is one of the oldest Franciscan friaries in Ireland. The walls are decorated with bird figures in homage to the founder of the order, St Francis of Assisi, and his love of animals. It was founded by Sir Hugh Purcell whose grandfather was a lieutenant to Strongbow who led the Anglo-Norman invasion of Ireland in 1170. It is believed that Purcell may have established the friary on behalf of King Henry III. Such a royal connection is reinforced by the location of the Franciscan friary itself: it is situated at the heart of the Viking Triangle near Reginald's Tower.

In 1394, King Richard II visited Waterford and held court in Greyfriars. It is also where four major Irish chieftains, the O'Conor Don, de Burgo, O'Brien and O'Kennedy surrendered to the king. In 1540 the friary was closed by Henry VIII when he severed links with Rome and established his own church. It was surrendered by John Lynch and in September 1541 was granted to Master Patrick Walsh as a site to start the Holy Ghost Hospital thus maintaining it as a pious institution. The following year, part of the precinct was given to David Baliff which probably led to the opening of Bailey's New Street between Reginald's Tower and the friary.

The medieval church was furnished with a large-scale crucifix (now lost) that separated the chancel from the congregation as well as altars dedicated to the Virgin Mary and the three Magi. It contained a statue of St Christopher, the patron saint of travellers. One can still see the 13th-century triple lancets (tall, narrow windows with a pointed arch at the top) on the east gable, and the 15th-century tower. The corbels of the chancel contain images of an owl, a duck and a rabbit. The Lady Chapel dates to the late 13th century and has a trefoil-headed lancet topped by a circular light. It is now home to 'King of the Vikings', the world's first virtual reality Viking experience.

Waterford man Luke Wadding joined the Franciscan order and became one of its most influential members in the 17th century. He created the official list of saints of the Catholic Church and fixed 17 March as the date for St Patrick's Day. In the 17th century Greyfriars was an asylum for the poor, and it continued to be used as a hospital well into the 19th century. In the latter half of the 17th century the east end of the monastery

was recommissioned as a church for the Huguenots (French Protestants) and thus became known as the French Church.

Medieval Museum

This award-winning museum opened in 2013 and is Ireland's first purpose-built museum devoted to the medieval period. The semi-circular faced cladding wrapping around the back of Christ Church Cathedral linking both the cathedral and Constitution Square is made from Dundry stone. This type of stone was used in the original construction of the medieval Christ Church and choristers' hall. On the gable of the museum is the 'Lady of Waterford' inspired by the image on a 13th-century belt mount found during excavations in the city. The structure is U-shaped because of the many buildings

521. Medieval Museum, Waterford.

that surround it. The building is a tremendous feat of design by architects Rupert Maddock, Bartosz Rojowski and Agnieszka Rojowska.

The museum houses the unique 'cloth-of-gold' vestments dating from the 1460s. They are made from Italian silk woven in Florence. The panels were embroidered in Bruges which was the centre of the medieval embroidery industry. The Waterford cloth-of-gold vestments are the only full set of medieval vestments to survive in northern Europe. The museum is also home to King Henry VIII's cap of maintenance and the charter roll of Waterford. Encased within the museum are medieval undercrofts, the 15th-century mayor's wine vault and the 13th-century chorister's hall. This hall was the lower floor of the deanery built in the 1270s by the warrior Bishop of Waterford and Governor of Ireland, Stephen de Fulbourn. The museum has a range of guided tours, multimedia presentations and informative displays showcasing the history of Waterford city.

Christ Church Cathedral

Waterford was granted its first bishop in 1096 but it is believed that the city's first cathedral was not built until after 1152. The original cathedral predates the Anglo-Norman invasion but was refurbished in 1210. It was the location of the marriage of Strongbow and Aoife which entwined the histories of Ireland and Britain for the best part of 800 years. In the 13th century, the Anglo-Normans built a Gothic cathedral that remained in place until the present Christ Church was constructed (beginning in 1773). The layout of the medieval cathedral can be gleaned from numerous illustrations and a plan. It had a central nave and

chancel with an aisle on either side and extended to the east with a tower to one side. Chapels were then added over the following centuries. Archaeologist Dave Pollock notes: '[t]he floor level of the old cathedral is well below the present granite slabs. A decorated pier of the medieval building can be seen, standing on a mortar floor 1.8m down. The plain finish on the old floor may overlie paving or tiles'.

The present cathedral was designed by John Roberts in the 1770s containing portions of the earlier church from 1210, such as the remains of an Anglo-Norman cluster pillar. It is believed that Bishop Chenevix was reluctant for a new cathedral to be constructed in a Georgian style, so a little ruse was used

522. Christ Church Cathedral, Waterford.

to 'help' him change his mind. Some potential builders arranged for rubble to fall in his path as he walked through the cathedral. After a couple of narrow escapes Chenevix decided that a new cathedral was a necessity. Gunpowder was used in the demolition of the medieval cathedral.

The neo-Classical cathedral, made primarily from limestone, was completed in 1779 at a cost of £5,397. It is made up of an eight-bay double-height nave and a single-bay four-stage tower towards the entrance. Roberts was a proponent of architectural design which echoed that of ancient Greece. His original interior has been altered substantially, due in part to a fire in the organ gallery in 1815.

The interior was remodelled by Sir Thomas Drew in 1891. The square pews and galleries were removed and the ground floor windows blocked up. In addition, a new case for the organ was constructed. In 2003 the organ was restored and located at a new gallery in its original location. The Elliot organ was commissioned in 1817, then placed in a corner of the cathedral after the late-19th-century remodelling. It has a solid mahogany case containing gold-plated pipes and is considered one of the finest organs in the country outside of Dublin. Visitors can also view the Gothic cadaver tomb of James Rice, Mayor of Waterford on eleven occasions during the 15th century. He built a chapel to house his tomb in the original Anglo-Norman cathedral. Since the construction of the current cathedral his tomb, which he shares with his wife Katherine Broun, has been moved on two occasions,

523. The opening meet of the hunt, The Mall, November 1928.

occupying its present position since 1880. The tomb's message is reflected in the Latin inscription on it which translates: 'I am what you will be; I was what you are now'.

John Condon Memorial

Unveiled on 18 May 2014 at Cathedral Square, the 4-metre-high John Condon Memorial was sculpted by Pat Cunningham. Private John Condon from Ballybricken died at Bellevarde Ridge in the Second Battle of Ypres, Belgium on 24 May 1915. His headstone records that he was fourteen years old and because of this it was long believed that he was the youngest British soldier to die in the First World War. It is now known that he was eighteen years old at the time of his death. He was known as the 'boy soldier' and what is traditionally believed to be his grave at Poelkapelle Cemetery in Belgium is much visited. Around 4,800 men from Waterford city and county fought in the First World War with over 1,100 dying in the conflict.

The Mall

Developed in the 18th century, the Mall (meaning walkway or promenade) stretches from Reginald's Tower to Colbeck Street. It was previously known as Miller's Marsh due to its being the location of Colbeck's Mill and mill pond. The mill pond took up a large portion of the present Mall. The mill was situated south-east of Reginald's Tower and an early reference to it as the 'Mill of Caldebec' dates to around 1224. It subsequently came into the hands of the Knights Templar, being leased to Walter le Devneys in 1326. After the Suppression of the Monasteries by Henry VIII in the 1540s it came into the

ownership of William Wyse.

From the early 18th century the idea of creating a bowling green and walking area was under consideration by the corporation. The Bowling Green (to be used by members only) was eventually launched in 1735. It was located at Rose Lane on the north segment of the Mall. The development of the Mall began in 1737 (now referred to as the 'Old Mall'). It was lined with elm trees on either side. By 1781, the corporation was considering using the area of the Bowling Green for an assembly rooms and playhouse but decided on the other side of the Mall. The construction of both buildings was completed by 1788. One of the first civic events held at the Assembly Rooms was a breakfast for Prince William Henry, the future King William IV.

In 1816, the Corporation moved from the Exchange on the Quay to the Assembly Rooms to hold council meetings. From then on the building was referred to as the Town Hall.

33 The Mall

Built in the late Georgian period, this was a townhouse for the Carew family before becoming the Wolfe Tone Confederate Club (the local headquarters of an Irish nationalist independence movement). A terraced single-bay, four-storey bow-fronted house was noted as the 'City's Meeting House of the Young Irelander movement' and is now better known for being the reputed location where the Irish tricolour of green, white and orange was first flown on 7 March 1848. On 15 April 1848, Waterford-born Thomas Francis Meagher was presented with the tricolour made from French silk and said:

I trust that the old country will not refuse this symbol of a new life from one of her youngest children. I need not explain its meaning. The quick and passionate intellect of the generation now springing into arms will catch it at a glance. The white in the centre signifies a lasting truce between the 'orange' and the 'green' and I trust beneath its folds, the hands of the Irish Protestant and the Irish Catholic may be clasped in generous and heroic brotherhood...

The building was extensively reconstructed in the 1970s. In the intervening years it has been a tobacconist's, a nightclub and a café.

524. 33 The Mall, Waterford.

People's Park

The People's Park is located at the junction of William Street and the Park Road. In 1855 the then Mayor of Waterford, John A. Blake, ordered that the marshland (known as Lombard's Marsh) by Newtown Road be used in creating a park. St John's River was again diverted in 1857 with the marshland drained to form the 16.3 acre park that exists today. The original design for the park was devised by the gardener, Mr Nevin. The park was inaugurated when it hosted the Royal Agricultural Show in August 1857. It was finally completed by November 1857.

The secretary of the Park Committee, Lieutenant-Colonel Roberts, addressed the crowd at the park's opening by saying that 'while this Park falls short in magnitude and appearance of many constructed for similar purposes in other parts of the kingdom, it is a source of pride that it is the only one in Ireland of a People's Park'.

On the grounds of the People's Park are a Victorian bandstand (erected in 1869), the Goff cycle track (dating to 1891) and a children's playground. There is an iron bridge connecting the park to the courthouse. The old caretaker's house is now the Park Lodge Café. Visitors can see two Russian guns by the bandstand which date to the Crimean War. In 1883 an ornamental fountain was added to the park but it was vandalised in 1977 and again in the early 1980s, this time beyond repair. A small fountain with a sphere can be seen in its place today. In 2006, the People's Park received €1 million funding for refurbishments and the development of a skateboarding park.

525. The People's Park, Waterford.

City Hall

Construction of City Hall began in 1783. It was designed by the architect John Roberts originally as an assembly rooms where the merchant classes could gather. The first ball held there was on 4 August 1785. It was subsequently agreed that the mayor would have the use of the building's first floor to stage public events. The nine-bay, two-storey building contains a committee room, the council chambers and a large room (completed in 1788) for civic engagements. The Council Room contains a cut-glass chandelier manufactured by Waterford Glass, a copy of which is in the Hall of Independence in Philadelphia, USA.

The Large Room was originally devised as a ballroom, hence the gallery which is in the room for orchestras. The 1798 Rebellion saw the North Cork Militia being billeted in the Assembly Rooms. Notable figures to speak at the Large Room over the centuries include Daniel O'Connell, the American social reformer Frederick Douglass, Charles Stewart Parnell and Patrick Pearse.

The building now houses an exhibition entitled 'The Mayors' Treasury' which showcases twenty-three objects ranging from 1080 to the present day, tracing the history of the mayoralty in the city, Roger le Lom being the first recorded mayor in 1284.

526. 'The Mayors' Treasury' in the foyer of City Hall celebrates a civic administration that stretches back to the foundation of the city in the 10th century.

Theatre Royal

This Victorian horseshoe theatre within a recently-restored Georgian building is Ireland's oldest continually operating theatre. Opened in 1785, the first play to be staged here was Shakespeare's *As You Like It*. Some well-known figures of 18th-century theatre to tread the boards of the Theatre Royal include the 'Swedish Nightingale' Jenny Lind and Catherine Hayes, the Limerick-born prima donna of La Scala in Milan. Local-born Shakespearean actor Charles Keane performed at the theatre in 1836. In 1876, the building was upgraded to the auditorium which exists today. On the opening night the theatre was unable to deal sufficiently with the large crowd who wanted to enter it. This led to some women fainting as a crush began and the police were needed to bring order to proceedings. The first act to perform in the new Theatre Royal was John Royston's comedy and opéra bouffe. The year 1882 saw smoking prohibited in the theatre on pain of a £2 fine. A fine of £5 was levied on those who behaved in a 'foul or filthy' manner.

In the early 20th century, up until 1906, the Theatre Royal primarily staged musicals. Notable acts included Percy French and John McCormack. In 1910, John Collins leased the theatre for cinematograph performances. He was followed by Lawrence and Martin Breen who operated the Theatre Royal as both a cinema and theatre. The Buffalo Bill Cody Show performed on the stage where it is alleged that they shot the lights out at the end of their act. The Nobel prizewinning playwright Harold Pinter also performed on the theatre's stage.

However, by 1955 the Theatre Royal had fallen into financial difficulties and was deemed not viable by some in the civic administration of the city. This led to the creation of the Theatre Royal Society in 1956 to save the historic theatre. It reopened in March 1958 with a play about Irish nationalist Roger Casement with Cyril Cusack in the lead role. Cusack commented on the night that '[i]n serving our Irish theatre we endeavour to preserve the spirit of art and liberty for all our citizens. This is why it is our privilege to be called on to re-open the Theatre Royal as a national provincial centre of drama with the premiere of a play concerned with the spirit of liberty'. Considered the 'people's theatre', since it reopened the Theatre Royal has played host to the Festival of Light Opera, Féile na Scoileanna, Tops of the Town and the Waterford Pantomime Society. Waterford-born Tony Award-winning actress Anna Manahan also reprised her role here in Martin McDonagh's *The Beauty Queen of Leenane*.

After an extensive renovation overseen by director Ben Barnes, the Theatre Royal reopened in 2009 with the staging of a Bernard Farrell play entitled *Wallace, Balfe and Mr Bunn*. In 2014, to coincide with the 1,100th anniversary of the founding of Waterford, an opera composed by Eric Sweeney and Mark Roper was performed entitled *The Invader*.

527. Bishop's Palace, Waterford.

Bishop's Palace

The location of the Bishop's Palace has been a dwelling-place for the Bishop of Waterford since 1096 when the city obtained its first bishop. In 1743, architect Richard Castle drew up the original drawings for the palace but work never began and the project was given to Waterford architect John Roberts.

In 1820, Richard Darcy was the head gardener for the grounds of the palace and his wife was working as a maid there. Richard Darcy's brother James visited the palace intent on killing Richard and his wife to obtain their savings as his inheritance. Over the course of two weeks he proceeded to poison the couple with arsenic while telling the staff of the palace that the pair had contracted cholera. Dr Thomas Lewis Mackesy uncovered the plot by questioning all the staff and discovering the vestiges of the poison. James Darcy was subsequently hanged for the crime. The palace was the home of successive Church of Ireland Bishops of Waterford and Lismore until the early 20th century when it became a school and later council offices. The Bishop's Palace is now a museum housing artefacts relating to Georgian, Victorian and 20th-century Waterford. Exhibits include a wide array of paintings, silver and glassware including the oldest known surviving piece of Waterford Crystal.

1916 Memorial

The 1916 Memorial consists of a bronze replica of the Proclamation of the Irish Republic read by Patrick Pearse at the commencement of the Easter Rising in 1916. It was erected in 2016 to commemorate the centenary of the Rising which had a defining and long-lasting effect on the island of Ireland. The monument was cast in a foundry in Brittany, France.

Strongbow and Aoife sculpture

To mark the 844th anniversary of the marriage of Strongbow and Aoife, these bronze sculptures were installed in 2014 to acknowledge the event that symbolised the histories of Britain and Ireland becoming entwined for the next eight centuries. The design is by Eithne Ring and Liam Lavery. It offers a fun photo opportunity for visitors to Waterford.

Constitution Square

In 2017, to mark the 80th anniversary of the signing of Bunreacht na hÉireann (the Irish Constitution) which was drafted by Waterford man John Hearne, the space between Christ Church Cathedral and the Bishop's Palace was named Constitution Square. Hearne later became Irish ambassador to the United States (1950-60) and began the tradition of presenting the US President with a bowl of shamrock on St Patrick's Day. A bust of Hearne was unveiled on 1 July 2017.

Waterford Crystal

The Waterford Glass Factory was established in 1783 by George and William Penrose at a cost of £10,000. The initial workforce numbered fifty to seventy staff. The work of John Hill was integral to the success of Waterford Glass. As a compounder, he devised the secret formula to make the glass and promoted polishing the glass after cutting for a frosted effect.

The ownership of the factory passed to Ambrose Barcroft, Johnathan Gatchell and James Ramsey in 1799, with Gatchell becoming the sole owner around 1810. The numbers employed at the factory had risen to between seventy and 100. It remained in the hands of the Gatchell family until 1851 when Waterford Glass ceased production.

In 1947, Czech immigrant Karel (Charles) Bacik set up Waterford Glass at Ballytruckle in Waterford city with around thirty blowers and cutters recruited from across Europe, one of whom, Miroslav Havel, was to have a defining effect on the designs of the new factory's crystal. After studying the patterns of the old glass factory, Havel created the Lismore pattern which became the most popular design of all Waterford glass.

The new factory expanded to Johnstown in the 1950s (recording its first profit in 1955) and then to Kilbarry in 1970, with the building finally completed in 1973. Waterford Crystal endured many financial highs and lows but producing the Times Square New Year's Eve Millennium Ball was undoubtedly a high point in the company's history. It was a great testament to the quality, tradition and the world renown of Waterford glass. The economic crash of 2008 greatly impacted Waterford Crystal leading to over 1,000 workers being laid off and a receiver being appointed. The company was eventually reborn and moved to its new city centre home on the Mall in 2010.

City walls

As Ireland's oldest city, the earliest references to the fortification of Waterford are in 1088 in the *Annals of Ireland.* Gerald of Wales also referred to the Hiberno-Norse defences when the city was captured by the Anglo-Normans in 1170. One of the attackers, Raymond le Gros, noted 'a small building overhanging the city wall supported on the outside by a beam'. It was attacked and when it collapsed it took a substantial part of the city wall with it, leading to the defeat of the Hiberno-Norse defenders. Over the following decades a significant wall-building programme was undertaken.

528. *The oldest surviving piece of Waterford Crystal, a decanter made in 1789.*

As Waterford extended west, no less than three new defensive city gates were built prior to 1212 under the reign of King John. By the end of the Middle Ages a complete structure of towers and stone walls enclosed the city.

By the early 18th century, the wall running along the Quay was demolished and today the remains of eight of the original thirty towers can be seen. They are:

The French Tower (situated at the top of Castle Street next to Brown's Lane).

The Double Tower (further down Castle Street), containing two interior chambers from which it derives its name. One of the chambers has a passageway to the nearby Benedictine priory of St John.

The cylindrical Watch Tower (at Manor Street) dating from the 13th century.

St Martin's Gate (Spring Garden Alley), one of three terminal posts of the original Viking city.

Reginald's Tower (at the apex of the Viking Triangle connecting the Mall and the Quay), Ireland's oldest urban civic building.

Turgesius' Tower (named after a Viking chief active in Ireland during the 9th century), the base of which was uncovered in 2009 during the redevelopment of Penney's department store.

The Beach Tower at Jenkin's Lane, one of the finest towers of the old city's defences with distinct 15th-century Irish crenellations. Previously neglected, the tower was restored, and buildings that had hidden it were removed in the 1990s to show off its impressive construction. Considerable credit is due to the work of archaeologist Ben Murtagh and the Waterford Civic Trust who aided the project financially.

The semi-lunar tower behind De La Salle on Patrick Street.

THE RAILWAY

Losing track: the life, death and rebirth of Waterford's railway.

he 19th century saw the golden age of railway and Ireland followed the lead of Britain in the drive towards rail travel for the masses. In the days before good road surfaces and motorcars, railways made long-distance travel fast, efficient and comfortable for the first time. In terms of its impact, it was arguably as significant as the invention of the internet. Ordinary individuals now had the opportunity to travel from one end of the country to the other with relative ease. In the south of Ireland the dream was simple: to develop a trade route from Cork through Rosslare / Fishguard and on into Britain. It was envisaged that Ireland would see a boost in trade similar to that of Britain. Proponents of the railway line in Waterford expressed the view that it would be of great benefit to the landowners of the area.

When it came to railway plans and railway companies, Waterford, like every other part of Ireland, was certainly not short of them. There were so many companies that it is easy to mix up their names or more importantly their acronyms, which were in general usage. In 1845 there was the C&WR (Cork and Waterford Railway Company) which planned to develop seventy-five miles of railway line from Cork to Waterford, via Youghal and Dungarvan. For financial reasons the line never went further than Youghal and so in 1854, the company was renamed the C&YR (Cork and Youghal Railway Company).

Other plans followed and in 1865 the WL&FR (Waterford, Lismore and Fermoy Railway Company) was also given permission to construct railways from Waterford to Dungarvan and from Fermoy to Lismore. The line from Dungarvan to Lismore was to have been built by the CL&DR (Clonmel, Lismore

602. A steam train crossing the Causeway, Abbeyside in the direction of Dungarvan Station c.1900.

and Dungarvan Railway). Unfortunately, both the WL&FR and the CL&DR had problems getting members of the public to invest in them and so the line from Clonmel to Dungarvan was never constructed. Constructing a railway line was both expensive and politically tricky. Each line required the passing of an Act of Parliament before any money could be secured. In the case of the WL&FR, it was noted that: '[n]o part of the Capital of the said Company has been subscribed, and there is no likelihood of any of the said Capital being subscribed'. Not much of an endorsement of the railway plan, given that the 1865 Act allowed for a total subscription of £400,000.

To encourage investment in risky railway projects, companies were often set up under a baronial guarantee. When the profits (where they existed) of a railway company were insufficient to pay a return to shareholders, shareholders would receive their dividends (share of the profits) through payments from the ratepayers in the district through which the railway company operated. The Waterford, Dungarvan and Lismore Railway line was funded under such a scheme.

WD&LR

The Waterford, Dungarvan and Lismore Railway Company (WD&LR) was incorporated in 1872, using £280,000 share capital plus a £93,333 loan from the Treasury. Due to the guaranteed 5% return on their investment over twenty-two years, people from all over the United Kingdom invested in the company. Many investors would never have visited Waterford and would have had no connections to the area. Just like today, 5% would have been regarded as a reasonable return on their investment, especially as their investment was relatively risk-free.

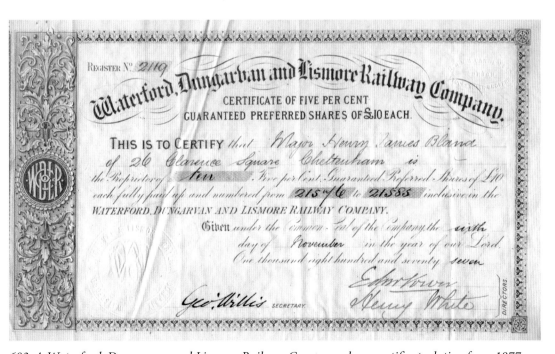

603. A Waterford, Dungarvan and Lismore Railway Company share certificate dating from 1877.

In 1873, under an amendment to the original Waterford, Dungarvan and Lismore Railway Act, 1872, the period of the baronial guarantee was extended from twenty-two years to a period of thirty-five years from the proposed opening of the line on 7 July 1878. Because the proposed railway line from Lismore to Waterford was to form part of an important trade route between the south of Ireland and Britain, an agreement was reached with the Great Western Railway Company of Great Britain (GWR) in relation to through fares and the amount to be paid for the use of the line. The agreement, which was reached in 1874, was eventually signed into law under the WD&LR Act, 1878. Under the agreement, the GWR agreed to pay a rebate of £1,000 per annum to the WD&LR on the condition that the money be put towards the payment of dividends and/or outstanding debt repayment. As goods traffic from Britain would pass over the line operated by the WD&LR, it was in the interests of the GWR

for the WD&LR to operate efficiently. The £1,000 annual rebate was a mutually beneficial arrangement.

Construction of the railway

The WD&LR constructed 43¾ miles of railway between Lismore in the west of the county and Waterford city (Gracedieu) in the east. Construction of the line was broken into three divisions: division 1 from Waterford to Kilmacthomas, division 2 from Kilmacthomas to Dungarvan and division 3 from Dungarvan to Lismore. Divisions 1 and 2 were constructed by Messrs Smith, Finlayson and Ashwell, with division 3 constructed by Stanford. While it was also a shorter distance from Dungarvan to Lismore than the previous plan of 1845 (C&WR) to connect Dungarvan with Youghal, the fact that Lismore was also the Irish home of key investor the Duke of Devonshire may very well have sealed the deal. The Duke was previously responsible for constructing the railway line between Fermoy and

604. The staff of Dungarvan Station c.1930.

Lismore and it became known locally as the 'Duke's Line'. The Duke, as well as being a key investor in the WD&LR, also provided cheap funding for the initial leasing of trains or rolling stock. (Rolling stock refers to the locomotives, carriages, wagons or other vehicles used on a railway.)

Building the railway line from Lismore to Waterford city involved the construction of seven railway stations (Cappoquin, Cappagh, Dungarvan, Durrow, Kilmacthomas, Kilmeaden and Bilberry – Waterford South), three large viaducts (Ballyvoile, Durrow and Kilmacthomas), Ballyvoile tunnel, numerous other smaller bridges and gate lodges. The tunnel at Ballyvoile is 382 metres long and required some additional lining and considerable expense due to the porous nature of the rock.

The stone viaduct at Kilmacthomas consists of eight arches, each arch over 10 metres wide and an arch height of 20 metres from river level, with just over 2 metres between arches.

The stone viaduct at Durrow consists of seven arches, each arch over 10 metres wide and an arch height of 17.6 metres from river level, with just over 2 metres between arches. The viaduct at Ballyvoile had to be rebuilt after the Irish Civil War (1922-23) and was originally built entirely of stone.

At one point there were over 900 men and 100 horses involved in the construction of the railway line and in the days before the invention of the JCB, this was a massive undertaking and an impressive feat of engineering.

Too many standards

Nothing is standard when you have too many standards and this certainly applied to the railway gauge or track width. The Railway Regulation (Gauge) Act, 1846 specified a track width of 5 feet 3 inches in Ireland and 4 feet 8 inches in Britain. While greater gauges were in existence, the selections were based on the amount of track already laid in each country. A much narrower gauge of 3 feet (narrow gauge) also continues to be used in tourism and mining, due to the lower costs involved. A great example is the successful Waterford and Suir Valley Railway (W&SVR), which today operates a regular tourist train from Kilmeaden to Waterford city, along the route of the original railway line.

Perhaps the only flaw with Irish Standard Gauge was the extra cost and difficulty in sourcing locomotives, as any trains acquired from Britain would need to be manufactured to meet the Irish standard. The company could buy existing locomotives from a railway company in Ireland or have them built to order in Britain. For this reason the WD&LR initially provided a limited service of no more than two daily trains each way until the company acquired its own locomotives from Sharp, Stewart and Co. and was then in a position to run three trains per day. The original trains for the line were supplied at an expensive rate by the Dublin, Wicklow and Wexford Railway (DW&WR) and the GS&WR.

Finance for leasing the locomotives was provided at an inexpensive rate by the Duke of Devonshire, without which the line might not have opened on time.

Director Mr Power made the following statement regarding the initial cost of rolling stock:

Then we had laboured under the disadvantage that we had no rolling stock – no plant – and should either borrow or hire. We did hire at a very considerable rent one engine from the Great Southern and Western Company, and two from the Dublin, Wicklow, and Wexford Company. We paid an enormous rent for those engines. Well, we have been relieved from all that difficulty by the Duke of Devonshire ... We actually pay less to the Duke of Devonshire for the entire stock, with four engines, than we paid before for the three engines to the other companies.

K.A. Murray and D.B. McNeill record that '[t]he company eventually owned seven locomotives, twenty-one passenger vehicles and about 140 wagons. Six of the engines were 0-4-2s by Sharp, Stewart & Co. and the seventh, a 2-4-0T, had originally belonged to the C&YR'. (0-4-2 refers to the wheel arrangement (using the Whyte notation) of the trains. In this case the trains had two pairs of drive wheels (4) followed by a pair of smaller trailing wheels (2). By comparison the Flying Scotsman, arguably the world's most famous locomotive, has a wheel arrangement of 4-6-2.)

The opening of the line

The Board of Trade requested a number of alterations to the system and after a two day inspection by Colonel Rich, the railway line between Lismore and Waterford opened, albeit five weeks late, on 12 August 1878. Initially there were three classes of railway ticket, but this was later reduced to two.

605. A Waterford, Dungarvan and Lismore Railway ticket dating from 1891.

There were two trains each way run to-day at 7.20am and 3.20pm from Lismore to Waterford, and at 10am and at 2.50pm from Waterford to Lismore. Both journeys were accomplished without a single hitch, and all the stations were reached with great punctuality. (Cork Examiner, 13 August 1878)

Whilst waiting for the moment of starting, the spectators examined the different carriages, and were highly pleased with all, especially the second class, which are very comfortably cushioned, and are not inferior to anything of the kind in the three kingdoms. (Waterford News, 16 August 1878)

A look at the company accounts for this period shows that the company was pretty much reliant on all types of business. Whether it was the transportation of people, soldiers, livestock, crops or parcels (which included fish), a drop in any sector was a problem for the company. The railway

carried livestock to markets in Waterford city and Dungarvan and day-tripping tourists to the seaside.

The steam trains may now be gone, but the scenery enjoyed by visitors to the Greenway remains the same, as is evidenced by this description in the *Waterford News* of 14 June 1878:

The line on the margin of the Suir, up to Mount Congreve, is unusually picturesque and beautiful, and again in the shadow of the Comragh Mountains at Kilmacthomas, and near Dungarvan, the tourist will be reminded of some scenes which he has witnessed on the continent.

As with tourism, the transportation of animals was a seasonal affair, but it was also affected by animal health and the rise and fall of market prices as animals were scarce or plentiful. It depended very much on the availability of animals in relatively close proximity to the line.

606. *A goods train at the New Line, Abbeyside, 1967.*
(*Photo © Michael J. Walsh; reproduced courtesy of the Irish Railway Record Society.*)

Unlike today, it was not always possible for a farmer to travel a long distance with animals and the roads were not in a fit state to support such traffic. The railway provided cheaper animal fares around market days to boost trade at the markets and tourists also availed of discounted tickets in what was a massive boost to the industry. An example of the difference the new line made is that it was now possible to transport pigs from the market in Lismore to Waterford city by 9.30 a.m. the same morning. The previous route went via Fermoy, Mallow and Limerick Junction, cost three times more and did not arrive until the next day.

While we often associate coal with the railways, the railway was perhaps as much a transporter of coal as a consumer of it. The WD&LR had to compete with the ports of Waterford and Dungarvan when it came to trade: much of the county's coal supply, among other goods, came into the ports and did not necessarily require transportation on the railway.

The bottom line

The *Cambridge Dictionary* describes a crisis as a 'situation that has reached an extremely difficult or dangerous point; a time of great disagreement, uncertainty or suffering'. Whatever about suffering, by August 1879, just a year after the opening of the line, the WD&LR had most certainly reached a point of extreme difficulty and disagreement. With an accounting deficit of £124,932 the company was no longer in a position to pay shareholder dividends in advance of the guaranteed money from the 'county and city of Waterford'. A meeting of the shareholders was held on 27 August 1879, at which they were more

fully informed about the issues affecting the company. It appears that the cost of land acquisition and extra unplanned works may have led to the increased cost of construction. Unplanned works included:

- The reconstruction of the bridge at Cappoquin costing £13,600, which was partially destroyed by flooding on 27 September 1875.
- The extension of 'Whelan's bridge' near Kilmeaden costing £5,000.
- Unplanned earth and rock cutting costing £16,588.
- The alteration of Mount Congreve walls costing £2,962.
- Sea-pitching at Dungarvan costing £3,107.
- Changes on Colligan Bridge, Dungarvan costing £4,400.
- The arching of Ballyvoile tunnel with brick costing £7,200.

To put these costs into some sort of context, the average weekly railway traffic figures for that time of year – the peak summer period – amounted to £303. This of course would not take into account the cost of running the line. The company was very clearly in financial trouble.

The early 1880s were not much better for the company. Creditors were unhappy that shareholders would still get their money through the baronial guarantee even though the company's creditors would be at a loss. The Board of Trade on behalf of the British Treasury was also looking at the £1,000 annual rebate which the company received from the GWR, as a possible source for the payment of the £93,333 debt owed to the Treasury. Luckily for the WD&LR,

607. Passenger train crossing Ballyvoile viaduct, 1967.
(Photo © Michael J. Walsh; reproduced courtesy of the Irish Railway Record Society.)

the courts decided against the creditors and the Board of Trade gave up on its claim to the £1,000 rebate. The mid-1880s saw a falloff in trade in common with other Irish railways and by 1892 there was a serious drop in earnings for the company. This was partly due to a depression in the cattle trade, leading in turn to less demand for grain and feed. Around this time there was also a shortage of pigs in the area.

For sale: one railway line

Things began to look a bit brighter when the WD&LR took over the running of the Fermoy and Lismore Railway

Company (F&LR) from the GS&WR on 1 March 1893, having been previously approved and confirmed at a meeting of shareholders on 10 March 1891. It was deemed by the board to be 'beneficial and satisfactory' and meant increased receipts at a time when they were most needed. From a practical viewpoint ticketing was simplified and the journey was treated as one section of railway line from Fermoy to Waterford.

By 1897 the WD&LR was still in financial difficulty and the Treasury was considering a possible takeover of the company in an effort to recoup the outstanding debt owed to it. The directors of the WD&LR

were furious, having reached agreement with the Board of Trade only a year earlier that all net profits from the railway line should go into the relaying of the line. The Treasury eventually accepted an offer from the GWR and the GSWR to buy out the company. However, while a separate offer from the Fishguard and Rosslare Railways and Harbours Company (F&RR&HC) in July 1897 was still before Parliament, the GWR together with the GS&WR decided to withdraw their original offer in support of the F&RR&HC. The Fishguard company was still to be jointly owned by the GWR and the GS&WR. Apart from offering to buy out the £93,333 debt, the Rosslare company also had to perform additional works on the line within a specified time period. The board of the WD&LR was not too keen on the deal and lodged a petition against it. It eventually took a £7 12s 6d-per-share offer from the F&RR&HC

to gain their support. On 27 May 1898 an agreement was reached between the F&RR&HC, GWR and GS&WR under which the GWR would operate the Fishguard network on the British side and the GS&WR would operate the Irish side of operations. And so, on 12 August 1898, an Act of Parliament cleared the sale of the WD&LR – along with the F&LR – to the F&RR&HC. Together, the GWR and GS&WR now controlled the rail route between Cork and Britain. The WD&LR as a company was now gone.

Bridge over the River Suir

Perhaps surprisingly, the railway stations of Waterford South and Waterford North, on either side of the River Suir, were not connected by rail until a bridge was constructed by Scottish engineer Sir William Arrol in 1906. Waterford South would eventually be phased out, but the

608. A train crossing the bridge in Kilmacthomas, 1967.
(Photo © Michael J. Walsh; reproduced courtesy of the Irish Railway Record Society.)

dream of a direct connection between Cork and Rosslare had finally come true.

The fragmented network

At a national level the big question being asked during the latter half of the 19th century and into the 20th was whether the country's railway companies should be amalgamated. Fares and transport charges were deemed to be too high and were seen as an impediment to the growth of the Irish economy. The development of Irish railways, it could be argued, had not brought about the same kind of boom in the Irish economy as had happened in Britain. Dungarvan-born James F.X. O'Brien, MP for Cork city, stated before the UK Parliament in 1904 'that the railway rates and defective transit facilities generally constitute a serious bar to the national advancement of Ireland and should receive immediate attention from the government'.

Various governments over many years, while eager to exact some sort of control over the railways in an effort to bring about some positive changes, tended to be opposed to outright state ownership. Either the various governments did not see railway management as part of their role or they saw the railways as a rather difficult problem which was best left to others. Apart from everything else, the purchase of the railways by the state would also have been quite expensive. The only alternative was for the various railway companies to agree terms among themselves for a private amalgamation. What militated against this idea was the fact that the various railway companies were in a variety of different situations. Some were profitable and others were not. The structure of ownership also varied, with many being under baronial

609. A steam train at Dungarvan Station c.1950.

guarantee and it was not necessarily in the interests of the profitable companies to take over the running of loss-making operations.

Irish War of Independence (1919-21) and Civil War (1922-23)

Train services around the country were affected by the Irish War of Independence and the resulting Civil War. Trains carrying British soldiers were often the target of the Irish Republican Army (IRA). In Waterford, one locally famous action was the Durrow engagement on 3 March 1921. While accounts of the event vary, certainly in terms of casualties, it is clear that a train carrying jurors to Waterford city was held up in order to lure out British soldiers in response. From an IRA perspective it was reported that several British soldiers were killed and wounded from a total of several hundred; at least one IRA Volunteer, Andy Kirwan, was wounded. The IRA later dispersed under cover of darkness.

During the Irish Civil War the viaduct and road bridge at Ballyvoile were both blown up by the IRA on 4 August 1922, supposedly in order to prevent Free State troops from entering Dungarvan. Initially just a single arch of the railway viaduct was damaged, but in the days that followed the remaining arches collapsed. Reconstruction work on the viaduct began in August 1923 and it reopened in June 1924. The road bridge was saved by promptly supporting it with wooden props and this avoided substantial reconstruction costs. Events such as these were seen as arguments for closing stretches of railway around Ireland and there was also debate about who should pay for the reconstruction work.

Irish Railway Act, 1924

The Irish Railway Act, 1924 allowed for the amalgamation of railways throughout the Irish Free State and in 1925 the Great Southern Railways Company (GSR) was formed to manage the rail network. The

610. The Keohan family at the foot of Ballyvoile viaduct, c. 8 August 1922. The viaduct had recently been blown up by Republicans.

611. *The new Ballyvoile viaduct nears completion, 8 June 1924.*

612. *The new Ballyvoile viaduct, 24 June 1924.*

act also provided for the use of bilingual signage at railway stations. The Free State wanted to make a strong statement by having Irish names added to all signage. The Great Southern and Western Railway, which originally absorbed the WD&LR, was now being absorbed into the GSR.

The formation of CIÉ and the arrival of diesel trains

Córas Iompair Éireann (CIÉ) was formed in 1945 under the Transport Act, 1944 and became responsible for most public transport in Ireland (road and rail). Against the advice of the Milne Report, compiled by Sir James Milne, CIÉ decided to introduce diesel trains from the 1950s onwards. Still dealing with fuel shortages from the period of World War II, it was thought that the use of diesel locomotives would lead to a far more efficient and cost-effective rail network. However, this was not enough to make the network profitable and public subvention of the transport system is still required to this day.

The last train from Dungarvan Station

With the closure of the Waterford and Tramore Railway in 1960, an arguably far more viable service which was being replaced by a regular bus connection, it was not long before the Mallow to Waterford line faced a similar fate. The Tramore service was unconnected to any other railway and ran from Tramore to Waterford city. It brought tourists and day-trippers out from the city to the town of Tramore, which remains a popular seaside destination. By then, every rail service in Ireland found itself competing with improving bus services, more often than not operated by the same company, CIÉ.

According to the Minister for Transport and Power at the time, Eskine Childers, 'this railway is really a bus service forced to travel along railway lines'.

The last train service from Dungarvan occurred on Saturday 25 March 1967 at 8.20 p.m. Local photographer and journalist Tom Tobin described the scene in his column 'Behind the Spotlight' in the local *Dungarvan Leader* newspaper (1 April 1967):

The historic occasion did not go unnoticed for as the train passed through the level crossing at the Abbeyside Causeway a big number of cars pulled up on either side sounded their horns in salute and re-echoed the diesel engine's own peculiar [horn] being heard for the last time in these surroundings. About forty people boarded the train at Dungarvan and travelled with it as far as Durrow or Kilmacthomas...

Quigley Magnesite Factory

This factory, which was involved in the production of magnesite, opened at Ballinacourty, Dungarvan in 1970 and required a railway connection (spur) from the factory onto the original Mallow-Waterford line, so that dolomite and other materials could be brought between the factory and Bennettsbridge in Co. Kilkenny. The factory employed up to an estimated 150 people and closed in 1982. Not only was the closure a financial loss to the workers and to CIÉ, but also to the whole economy of Dungarvan. According to local TD Austin Deasy, '[t]he Quigley Magnesite industry paid out £1½ million annually in wages and salaries, plus another £3½ million in company contracts and purchases in the locality, while the operation is estimated at having been worth £1½ million to CIÉ per annum'.

The Waterford Greenway

While there were inspection locomotives running on the line from time to time during the 1980s, the railway from Lismore to Waterford, which was originally operated by the WD&LR, had now ceased operation for good. With the arrival of the Waterford and Suir Valley Railway (which operates a tourist train from Kilmeaden to Waterford) and the later opening of the Waterford Greenway, the line which was originally opened to serve the needs of a relative few, is now once again serving the masses. Rather appropriately, the opening date of the Waterford Greenway was 25 March 2017, fifty years to the day since the last passenger train left Dungarvan.

Further reading

Irish Railway Record Society: irishrailarchives.ie

Edmond Keohan, *Illustrated history of Dungarvan* (1924)

David Murray, 'Mallow to Waterford', *Journal of the Irish Railway Record Society*, 18/121 (June 1993), 236-51

K.A. Murray and D.B. McNeill, *The Great Southern and Western Railway* (1976)

Tom Tobin, *Echoes from the Decies: a Waterford scrapbook* (1953)

613. A crowded platform at Dungarvan Station c.1955.

Kilmacthomas viaduct.

Directory of Waterford history

Hopefully the contents of this book will have piqued your interest in Waterford history. I have compiled a directory of historical places and resources from around the county to help you explore further. For general questions about Waterford history I would recommend joining the Waterford History Group on Facebook. If you have a question about a particular place, contact the local history group associated with that locality. In addition to the resources listed below, most towns and villages in Waterford now have Facebook groups such as Things you miss about Dungarvan/Abbeyside and Kilmacthomas Photo Archive, Past and Present. These groups are particularly good at covering the recent history of their area.

Twitter

@CCUGeopark – the Copper Coast Geopark is an outdoor museum of geological records; it stretches along the coast from Kilfarrasy to Stradbally, Co. Waterford.

@Gallowshill2018 – Waterford County Museum's community archaeology project. Tweets by Christina Knight-O'Connor.

@IrishSmuggling – Waterford-based historian specialising in Irish smuggling.

@LismoreHC – Lismore Heritage Centre is a visitor centre and tourist office. It also offers guided tours and school tours.

@tidesntales – researching the maritime heritage of the 'Three Sisters' rivers (Barrow, Suir and Nore) and Waterford harbour.

@Odubhlainn – Simon Dowling from Waterford city specialises in photogrammetry and aerial archaeology.

@WaterfordLibs – twelve Waterford library branches dedicated to reading, education, culture and community.

@waterfordmuseum – Dungarvan-based volunteer-run museum preserving Co. Waterford's history. Tweets by Willie Whelan.

@WfdHistSty – the Waterford Archaeological and Historical Society, publishers of the historical journal Decies.

@WFORD_Treasures – three visitor attractions in the Viking Triangle: the Medieval Museum, Bishop's Palace and Reginald's Tower.

Facebook groups

Ballymacarbry / Nire Historical Society – a local history group operating in the northernpart of the county, along the border with Tipperary.

Butlerstown and Kilmeaden History & Photo Archive – old images and historical information about people and places associated with Butlerstown and Kilmeaden.

Kilmacthomas Photo Archive, Past and Present – a photo archive of life in the village of Kilmacthomas.

Waterford History Group – the largest discussion group on Facebook for Waterford history. Admins are Dermot Power, Michael O'Sullivan, Tommy Deegan and Vinny O'Brien. Very knowledgeable contributors, particularly strong on Waterford city history.

Waterford Maritime History – a mix of modern and historical maritime information.

Waterford Railway History – a group for enthusiasts/historians of Waterford railway history.

Facebook pages

Abbeyside History – history and news from Abbeyside. Hosted by Eddie Cantwell and Christina Knight-O'Connor.

Ardmore Grange Heritage Group – founded to preserve, protect and promote the rich and diverse heritage of Ardmore and Grange.

Ballyduff Upper History & Heritage Club – a community-run club preserving the history of Ballyduff Upper.

Barony of Gaultier Historical Society – this group focuses on the coastal villages of Cheekpoint, Passage East and Dunmore East.

Cappoquin Heritage Group – preserving and promoting awareness of Cappoquin's rich local heritage in as many ways as possible. A non-profit voluntary group under the umbrella of Cappoquin Civic Link.

Copper Coast Geopark – the Copper Coast UNESCO Geopark is famed for its geological and mining heritage and rugged coastline. Discover more at the Geopark Visitor Centre.

Déise Medieval – a Waterford-based amateur society for living history and medieval combat enthusiasts.

Lismore Heritage Centre – housed in the old Lismore Courthouse it offers visitors and locals a unique insight into Lismore's rich history.

Mallow Fermoy Lismore Waterford Railway & Branch Lines – recording the railway, past and present, with text, photographs and maps.

Portlaw Heritage Centre – helping to protect and preserve the history of Portlaw.

Stradbally, Co. Waterford – Present and Past – a community archive for Stradbally, recalling times past and recording times present.

Waterford Archaeological and Historical Society – publishers of the historical journal Decies. The society organises an annual lecture series from September to May as well as historical outings in the summer months.

Waterford City and County Archive – the local authority archive for the city and county of Waterford. The archive collects archives and records of the history and development of the city and county and provides access to these records to the public.

Waterford Civic Trust – a voluntary organisation whose purpose is the enrichment, preservation, protection, promotion and improvement of heritage in Waterford city.

Waterford County Museum – Dungarvan-based volunteer-run museum preserving Co. Waterford's history.

Waterford Treasures – three museums in the Viking Triangle, the historic quarter of Ireland's oldest city.

Places to visit

Waterford has many interesting heritage attractions. The list below runs from west to east. As many of the locations are run by volunteers or open on a seasonal basis, contact the venue to determine opening hours.

Lismore Heritage Centre
Lismore,Co. Waterford.
Phone: +353 (0)761 102157
Web: www.discoverlismore.com
Offers a unique insight into Lismore's rich history and all the attractions it has to offer. The centre has recently been refurbished but retains the charm and history of the old courthouse building it is housed in.

Lismore Castle Gardens
Lismore,Co. Waterford.
Phone: +353 (0)58 54061
Web: www.lismorecastlegardens.com
The seven-acre historic gardens of Lismore Castle afford spectacular views of the castle and surrounding countryside. The castle itself is not open to the public.

Waterford County Museum
St Augustine Street,Dungarvan,Co. Waterford.
Phone: +353 (0)58 45960
Web: www.waterfordmuseum.ie
This award-winning community-run museum has a permanent exhibition on the history of Dungarvan and West Waterford. School and tour groups are welcome. Free admission.

King John's Castle
Castle Street,Dungarvan,Co. Waterford.
Phone: +353 (0)58 48144
Dungarvan Castle is an Anglo-Norman fortification founded in 1185. A restored 18th-century military barracks houses an informative exhibition on the history of the castle.

Woodhouse Museum
Woodhouse,Stradbally,Co. Waterford.
Phone: +353 (0)87 9644402
Located in the former stables, the Woodhouse Museum documents the history of the house and estate as well as the Stradbally area. To visit, make an appointment with the curator, Marianna Lorenc, at the above number
or at boudica35@gmail.com.

Copper Coast Geopark Visitor Centre

Knockmahon,Bunmahon,Co. Waterford.
Phone: +353 (0)51 292828
Web: www.coppercoastgeopark.com
Located in a restored 19th-century church, the Geopark Visitor Centre contains a local mining and environmental heritage exhibition, walking trail guides and leaflets as well as a high-quality café.

Curraghmore House

Portlaw,Co. Waterford.
Phone: +353 (0)51 387101
Web: www.curraghmorehouse.ie
Curraghmore House is the historic home of the Marquess of Waterford. Some 2,500 acres of formal gardens, woodland and grazing fields make this the largest private demesne in Ireland.

Portlaw Heritage Centre

Malcomson Square,Portlaw,Co. Waterford.
Phone: +353 (0)86 8364925
Web: www.portlawheritage.ie
This community-run heritage centre focuses on the industrial, social and cultural history of Portlaw. Free admission.

Waterford and Suir Valley Railway

Kilmeaden Station,Kilmeaden,Co. Waterford.
Phone: +353 (0)51 384058
Web: www.wsvrailway.ie
This narrow gauge family-friendly heritage railway runs along the picturesque banks of the River Suir.

Mount Congreve

Kilmeaden, Co. Waterford.
Phone: +353 (0)51 384 115
Web: www.mountcongreve.com
Mount Congreve is an 18th-century Georgian estate and mansion. The gardens consist of around seventy acres of intensively planted woodland garden and a four-acre walled garden.

Waterford Treasures Medieval Museum

Cathedral Square,Viking Triangle,Waterford.
Phone: +353 (0)761 102501
Web: www.waterfordtreasures.com

Ireland's only purpose-built medieval museum and the only building on the island to incorporate two medieval chambers, the 13th-century choristers' hall and the 15th-century mayor's wine vault.

Bishop's Palace Museum

The Mall, Viking Triangle, Waterford.
Phone: +353 (0)761 102501
Web: www.waterfordtreasures.com
This exquisite architectural jewel, now a museum focused on Georgian Waterford, continues to delight over 250 years after it was built. The ground and first floors are furnished as a very elegant 18th-century townhouse.

Reginald's Tower Museum

The Quay, Waterford.
Phone: +353 (0)761 102501
Web: www.waterfordtreasures.com
Reginald's Tower is Waterford's landmark monument and Ireland's oldest civic building. The tower now houses an exhibition on Viking Waterford.

The House of Waterford Crystal

The Mall, Waterford.
Phone: +353 (0) 51 317000
Web: www.waterfordvisitorcentre.com
Offering guided factory tours that allow you to witness how Waterford Crystal pieces are crafted.

Irish Railway Record Society

Founded in 1946, the Irish Railway Record Society caters for all who are interested in Irish railways and tramways. The society's journal, published three times a year, records the history of Irish railway and tramway transport, along with comprehensive coverage of current developments. Regular meetings are held in Dublin, Cork and London for presentations on historical and current affairs, with slides, films and DVDs. Dublin meetings are normally held on the second and fourth Thursdays of each month during the winter months at the society premises at Heuston Station, where the society's library, archives and small exhibit displays are also located.
Web: www.irrs.ie
Facebook: Irish Railway Record Society
Twitter: @irishrailways

Contributors

Eddie Cantwell

Long-time Waterford County Museum member Eddie Cantwell is the current Vice-President of the museum. Eddie's wide range of interests include local history, genealogy and graveyard research. Along with Christina Knight-O'Connor he initiated and manages the ongoing community archaeology project at Gallows Hill, Dungarvan for Waterford County Museum. He has published two books on local history, The way it was: *Ballinacourty, Ballinroad and Clonea: the families and their history* and *Garranbane Church: a history, 1807-2007*, and has contributed to three more. He has written historical articles for several magazines including *Beam*, the journal of the Irish lighthouse service. Since 2009 he has researched and published around 3,000 words of local history each week in the *Dungarvan Leader* newspaper. Eddie enjoys the local newspaper medium and maintains that it is a 'fast, effective, economic way of getting history out there [and that] it has an important role to play in bringing local history to people'. Along with Christina Knight-O'Connor he hosts the Abbeyside Heritage Archive online. Eddie also hosts two other blogs: one is about Ring and the other is about Dungarvan emigrants to the Isle of Wight. Eddie has documented the gravestones of twenty Waterford graveyards and contributed them to the website historicgraves.com. In his spare time he likes to read. He lives with his wife May at Kilminion South, Dungarvan.

Ger Crotty

Ger Crotty was born in Portlaw and educated at Portlaw National School and Mount Sion CBS. He works as a maintenance planner with Sanofi in Waterford. In 2007 he obtained a BA in History and Sociology from University College Cork as part of the Oscail programme. He served as an officer in the Reserve Defence Forces from 1993 to 2007 with a total of twenty-eight years service. His thesis on the Kilmacthomas Poor Law Union was published in *Decies* and he has delivered lectures on Portlaw and its past. Both Ger and the Portlaw Heritage Centre acknowledge the excellent research on Portlaw's social, industrial and built heritage carried out by researchers such as Tom Hunt, Majella Walsh and

Bill Irish among others. Ger is currently researching the impact of the Great War on Portlaw. An active member of the Portlaw Heritage Centre, he has served as Chairperson over the last number of years and also served as Chairperson of the Waterford City and County 2016 Commemoration Committee. He is currently Chairperson of the Waterford City and County 2018 Commemoration Committee. Ger lives in Portlaw with his wife Bernie.

Cian Flaherty

Cian Flaherty was born in Dublin but grew up in Stradbally, which he considers home. He graduated from Trinity College Dublin with a BA in History in 2018. He has an abiding interest in the history and culture of mid-Waterford and is in the process of compiling a survey of the old graveyard in Stradbally. He is Secretary of the Stradbally Church Ruins Committee which is charged with conserving Stradbally's medieval parish church. He is also involved with the Stradbally Photographic Archive, a new project which is gathering old and new photographs from Stradbally and district. Contact cianflaherty96@gmail.com for more information on any of these projects.

Cian would like to thank: Garvan Cummins, Seán, Judy and Ross Flaherty, John Galloway (for writing the Copper Coast section), Tom Hickey, Christine King, Marianna Lorenc, Luke O'Connor (for lending a hand with some rigorous copy-editing), Boyer Phelan, Elizabeth Quinn, and most importantly Blánaid ní Bhraonáin for her constant help and encouragement.

William Fraher

William Fraher is a local historian with a particular interest in architecture and the decorative arts. He is curator of Waterford County Museum and has written a number of publications and articles on the history of Dungarvan and Co. Waterford. Books authored or co-authored by William include *Dungarvan: an architectural inventory, Desperate Haven: the Poor Law, Famine and aftermath in Dungarvan Union* and *Dungarvan: historic guide and town trail.* He is a regular contributor to *Decies.* In 2017 a civic reception was held by Waterford Council at the Civic Offices, Dungarvan in recognition of William's enormous contribution to preserving the history of Dungarvan and Co. Waterford.

Christina Knight-O'Connor

Christina Knight-O'Connor has been a committee member of Waterford County Museum and Abbeyside Heritage Archive for eight years. Her interest in history was inspired from an early age by her grandmother and local historian, the late Ann Allridge. Christina's particular local history interests include social history, women's history and archaeology. In 2014, Christina co-researched the Revolutionary Waterford Women's Project with Eddie Cantwell, documenting the contributions and forgotten stories of Waterford women from 1916 to 1923. The research, which is ongoing, has been included in many local exhibitions and publications. In 2015, she co-ordinated a Waterford community archaeology project, working with local volunteers, professionals and state bodies to investigate the archaeology of Dungarvan and the surrounding area. The project's successful excavations at Gallows Hill have uncovered a lost 12th-century Anglo-Norman castle and evidence of conflict during the sieges of 17th-century Dungarvan. The project members are active participants in other nationally significant archaeological research investigations, including the Dungarvan Valley Caves Project, which is searching for evidence of Ireland's earliest human habitation. In 2016 Gallows Hill was selected as one of four sites in Ireland for the Heritage Council's Adopt a Monument initiative. The project was also awarded the Waterford PPN Community Culture Award in 2017 and the National Lottery County Heritage Award in 2018. Christina has contributed and presented research papers and articles to various conferences and local and national publications. She is currently co-researching a social history book recording seventy years of T.J. Murphy Place, Abbeyside's first local authority housing development. The book is due to be published in 2019. Her qualifications include General Nursing and a BA (Hons) in Sociology. Christina is currently in the final year of studying Archaeology at NUI Galway and looks forward to continuing to pursue her interest and passion for local history and the hidden archaeology of Co. Waterford.

Cian Manning

Cian Manning was educated at Mount Sion Primary and Secondary School in Waterford city and studied at University College Cork. He has contributed articles to *Ireland's Own*, Headstuff, Póg Mo Goal and the *Waterford News and Star*. Cian has been a committee member of the Waterford Archaeological and Historical Society since 2012 and the Hon. Editor of the society's journal *Decies* for issues 72 to 74.

Cian would like to thank: his parents Oliver and Miriam Manning and brother

Olin for all their support. The Waterford Archaeological and Historical Society. Peigí Devlin for her help, advice and sharing her knowledge. Cian Flaherty, Julian Walton and Willie Whelan for their help and expertise, greatly appreciated. Donnchadh Ó Ceallacháin for his pointers and direction with images and information. Waterford Treasures.

Seán and Síle Murphy

This husband-and-wife team of local historians have been researching the local stories of the Comeraghs, Kilmacthomas and Co. Waterford for well over forty years and have accumulated a vast store of written material on diverse topics of social interest. They have been actively involved in the cultural life of mid-Waterford during this time. Síle Murphy Walsh is a retired national teacher who taught in the village school in Kilrossanty. Being a native of the Comeraghs and the last person to have been born in the townland of Coumshingaun, her knowledge of the mountains in folklore and legend is second to none. Her husband Seán comes from nearby Kilmacthomas but has lived in the mountains for over forty years. As a social welfare officer serving West Waterford, he absorbed a vast store of the lore of Co. Waterford and the Comeraghs. As the pension officer he had to interview many veterans of the War of Independence, collecting valuable historical information in the process. Seán and Síle have four children: Jack, Bob, Lia and Mahon.

Publications by the Murphys include: *The Comeraghs: Holy Year Cross* (1973), *The Comeraghs: fact and fancy* (1974), *The Comeraghs: fact and famine* (1975), *The Comeraghs: refuge of rebels* (1980), *The Comeraghs: famine, eviction and revolution* (1996), *Waterford: heroes, poets and villains* (1999) and *The Comeraghs: gunfire and civil war* (2003).

Julian Walton

Julian Walton is a former secondary schoolteacher and librarian with a lifelong interest in Irish history and genealogy, particularly relating to Co. Waterford. During the 1990s he worked at Waterford Heritage Genealogical Centre, where among other assignments he undertook the conservation of Waterford Cathedral Library. He was then employed at the library of University College Cork in the cataloguing of older printed books.

Since he 'retired' in 2006 he has been Resident Historian at Dunhill Multi-Education Centre in Co. Waterford, where he lectures on aspects of local history. He is the author of The Royal Charters of Waterford and of many articles in historical journals, especially *The Irish Genealogist* and *Decies*, and is a former editor of both journals. His most recent publications are *On This Day* volumes one and two, which comprise historical snippets based on a series which he presented on Waterford Local Radio between 1994 and 2012.

He is currently researching the history of Curraghmore with the assistance of William Fraher and Marianna Lorenc. He is also an active member of the Bookplate Society.

Martin Whelan

Martin Whelan is a computer programmer with an interest in the history of Waterford railway. He wrote the software and developed the information architecture for the Waterford County Museum website, the main component of which is the image archive. The museum website was shortlisted alongside four other museums – the Tate, Smithsonian, American Museum of Natural History and the University of Alberta – in the Best Research Site category at Museums and the Web 2002. It won Best Publication for Visitors at the Irish Museum of the Year Awards 2002 and Best Small Museum Website 2006 at the Museums and the Web International Conference in Albuquerque, New Mexico. The archive continues to grow and he plans to develop the site further when he gets some spare time.

Martin would like to thank: the staff of The National Archives (UK) for providing excellent access to original records. County Archivist Joanne Rothwell for her help with access to the Devonshire Papers relating to the railway. His brother Willie Whelan for annoying him to finish the railway chapter. His late father Paddy Whelan for helping him find all the railway stations and last remaining bits of track and infrastructure.

Willie Whelan

A native of Abbeyside now living out a happy exile in Colligan, Willie Whelan's family links to Abbeyside date back at least to the 1830s. A member of Dungarvan Museum Society since 1994, Willie initiated the society's name change to Waterford County Museum. He has co-authored *Desperate Haven: the Poor Law, Famine and aftermath in Dungarvan Union*, and two editions of *Dungarvan: historic guide and town trail*. The museum website, developed with his brother Martin, won Heritage Council Publication of the Year in 2002. In 2006, Best Small Museum

Website was awarded to the museum at the International Museums and the Web Conference in Albuquerque, New Mexico. In 2016, Willie received the Person of the Year Award from Dungarvan and West Waterford Chamber of Commerce in recognition of his heritage work. Projects that Willie has initiated and managed for the museum include: fundraising for the museum's renovation,the Grattan Square Heritage Plaque Project, Dungarvan's heritage signage, the museum's epublishing on Kindle, the museum's social media accounts and this book. He was a committee member of the group that erected the Waterford World War I memorial in Dungarvan. In his spare time, he is Chairman of Abbeyside Scouts and PRO of St Pat's Juvenile GAA and Ladies' Football Club.

Willie would like to thank: Ian MacKaye, Bill Hicks, Mike Patton, Andrea Camilleri, Esbjörn Svensson, Henry Blofeld, Timothy Williams, Jim Shine, Paul Ryan, Lucinda Shrubb, John McGrath, Margaret Cleere, Seamus O'Neill, Eoin Leane, Richie Power, Turlough Ó Carthaigh, Alan Toft, Catherine Hickey, Kevin Hickey, Olivia Butler, Kevin Walsh, James Dalton, Caroline Dunne, Catherine Whelan, Paddy Whelan, John Whelan and especially Rosie, Katie, Paddy, Jack and Harry.

Eamonn Bolger

Eamonn Bolger lives in Waterford city. He is married to Caroline and has three children, three grandchildren and a dog! He is an LFC lover and photography addict.

John Foley

A photographer and filmmaker, John Foley likes to combine his passions for photography and video with a love of the great outdoors. His idea of relaxation is spending a day with friends in the mountains or kayaking on the coast of Co. Waterford. If you need imagery or film to promote your business contact John at www.johnfoleyimages.com. You can follow John on Twitter @johnfoleyimages.

Pat Kenealy

Pat Kenealy would like to thank his wife Martina and children Adam, Chloe and Emma for putting up with him constantly disappearing to take photos! He started taking photos at fourteen and his interest grew from there. He got a drone a few years ago which really opened up lots of new photo opportunities. Sunrise and sunset are his favourite times to photograph. Anyone wishing to purchase any of Pat's photos can contact him at kenealyp@yahoo.ie or you can follow him on Twitter @patrickkenealy.

Michael Power and Anne Lannon Power

Michael Power is an Abbeyside native with a lifelong interest in local history and archaeology. Recently retired, he is enjoying the opportunity to focus on other pursuits including music and calligraphy. Anne Lannon Power, originally from Thomastown in Co. Kilkenny, is an artist specialising in watercolour and lino print. The maps in this book were drawn by Michael with colours by Anne.

Image credits

Images credited to Waterford County Museum have been given to us by many different donors over the years. For logistical reasons it is not possible to credit each donor individually. At www.waterfordmuseum.ie you can see the thousands of images that we hold in our archive.

Dungarvan
Pat Kenealy: 001, 012, 013, 017, 018, 024
Waterford County Museum: 002, 003, 005, 006, 007 (Anthony Chearnley from The antient and present state of the county and city of Waterford by Charles Smith), 008, 009, 010 and 011 (Illustrated history of Dungarvan by Edmond Keohan), 015, 016, 020, 021
Willie Whelan: 004 (courtesy of Claíomh, www.claiomh.ie), 022
Michael Power and Anne Lannon Power: 014
Dave Pollock: 019 (Medieval Dungarvan by Dave Pollock,
www.waterfordarchaeologist.ie)

Abbeyside
Pat Kenealy: 101, 111, 119, 124
Waterford County Museum: 102, 103, 105 (Anthony Chearnley from The antient and present state of the county and city of Waterford by Charles Smith), 106, 107, 108, 109, 110, 113, 115, 117, 118, 120, 121, 123
Willie Whelan: 104 (courtesy of Claíomh, www.claiomh.ie), 116
Michael Power and Anne Lannon Power: 112
Michael J. Walsh: 114 (photo © Michael J. Walsh; reproduced courtesy of the Irish Railway Record Society)
John Foley: 122

Stradbally
Pat Kenealy: 201, 209, 221
Waterford County Museum: 202, 203, 205, 206, 207, 210, 211, 213, 217, 218, 219, 220, 222
Elizabeth Quinn: 204
Michael Power and Anne Lannon Power: 208
John Foley: 212, 214, 216
PJ Maher: 215
George Munday: 223

Kilmacthomas
Pat Kenealy: 301, 308, 316, 317,
Waterford County Museum: 302, 306, 309, 310, 311, 312, 314, 315, 318, 319, 320, 321
Andy Kelly: 303, 304, 305, 307
Michael Power and Anne Lannon Power: 313

Portlaw
Pat Kenealy: 401, 413, 414, 415, 417, 418, 419, 420, 421, 422
Waterford County Museum: 402, 403, 406, 407, 408, 416
National Library of Ireland: 404 (NLILCAB04065)
Andy Kelly: 405, 409, 410, 411
Michael Power and Anne Lannon Power: 412

Waterford
Eamonn Bolger: 501, 510, 516, 520, 522, 525, 527
Pat Kenealy: 502, 524
National Library of Ireland: 503 (NLI POOLEWP 2103), 504 (NLI POOLEWP 0527a), 509 (NLI POOLEWP 0111), 512 (NLI POOLEWP 0733)
Waterford County Museum: 505 and 506 (Anthony Chearnley from The antient and present state of the county and city of Waterford by Charles Smith), 507, 513, 514, 515, 519, 523
Waterford Treasures: 508, 521, 526, 528
Library of Congress: 511, 518
Michael Power and Anne Lannon Power: 517

The Railway
Waterford County Museum: 601, 602, 604, 609, 610, 611, 612, 613
Martin Whelan: 603, 605
Michael J. Walsh: 606, 607, 608 (photos © Michael J. Walsh; reproduced courtesy of the Irish Railway Record Society)

Other images
Contents: photo of Abbeyside Church by Pat Kenealy
Finding places: map of Waterford by Michael Power and Anne Lannon Power
Directory of Waterford history: photo of Kilmacthomas viaduct by Pat Kenealy.
Front cover clockwise from top left: Pat Kenealy, Pat Kenealy, Eamonn Bolger, John Foley
Back cover clockwise from top left: Pat Kenealy, Waterford County Museum, John Foley, © Michael J. Walsh (reproduced courtesy of the Irish Railway Record Society)